THE SHAKING

"An excellent read! Challenging! Encouraging! Inspiring!"

Peter Butt, Cornerstone.

"This is a book written with an unfading vision for a church which is internally relational, friendly to sinners, truly apostolic and prophetic – not only by what it says but by what it does. It's difficult to put down, because we've all wondered why we are being shaken so severely. Well, *The Shaking* is likely to tell you."

Gerald Coates, leader of the Pioneer Network.

"I consider John Noble to be one of the catalysts to bring apostolic New Testament ministry into mainstream Christianity. This book will bring you into a greater revelation of apostolic ministry and what it means to today's church.

Ed Delph, N.A.T.I.O.N.S.

"The future will not be more of the same – we need to get ready. That's the stark urgent message of this radical manifesto for followers of Jesus in the third millennium. Deeply challenging, visionary and prophetic – John Noble's best book yet!"

Dr Patrick Dixon – founder of the international AIDS agency ACET and director of Global Change Ltd.

"John Noble's radical vision of the kind of church needed for the future is earthed in the radical discipleship that he and his wife have embraced and lived over many years. And that's what gives this book the ring of truth. It's a book forged in the white-hot heat of experience."

Rev. Sue Hope, Hon. Canon of Sheffield Cathedral.

"The passion for a mature church experiencing both suffering and triumph is infectious."

Stuart Lindsell, Pioneer People.

"*The Shaking* is a classic and has a message the church desperately needs to hear."

Philip Mohabir.

"I am thrilled by John Noble's vision of a flexible church that goes to people where they are – and forms church round them."

Rev. Dr Michael Moynagh, Director, Centre for Futures Studies, St John's College, Nottingham, and author of Changing World, Changing Church.

The Shaking

*Turning the church inside out
to turn the world upside down*

JOHN NOBLE

MONARCH
BOOKS

Mill Hill, London and Grand Rapids, Michigan

First published by Monarch Books in the UK 2002,
Concorde House, Grenville Place,
Mill Hill, London, NW7 3SA.

Distributed by:
UK: STL, PO Box 300, Kingstown Broadway, Carlisle,
Cumbria CA3 0QS;
USA: Kregel Publications, PO Box 2607
Grand Rapids, Michigan 49501.

ISBN 1 85424 575 9 (UK)

British Library Cataloguing Data
A catalogue record for this book is available
from the British Library.

Book design and production for the publishers by
Bookprint Creative Services
PO Box 827, BN21 3YJ, England
Printed in Great Britain.

DEDICATION

To my lovely wife, our children and their partners who have helped keep us on the journey by their love and support. They have been "church" for us in a very special way. Also to the next generation, our grandchildren – all 15 of them – may they carry the torch lightening the darkness until Jesus comes.

Dad/Grandpa

ACKNOWLEDGEMENTS

Thanks to my daughter Ruth for the hours and hours of typing and not one complaint in spite of all the additions and corrections – you're a star! Thanks to the many friends who took time to read the various drafts and make constructive and helpful criticisms, particularly Stuart Lindsell, Martin Scott, Geoff Shearn, Neil Edbrooke, Dr Linda and Ian Wilson, Peter Butt, Tim Brawn, Jim Holl, Derek Brown, Ian Farr, and Tony Pullin. Thanks to Dale Gentry for his kind "foreword"; but also that encouraging prophetic word assuring me that this book would go all over the USA. Finally, thanks to Richard Roberts and Philip Iszatt for their excellent appendix contributions.

John Noble

CONTENTS

FOREWORD

In every arena, things are changing rapidly, including the church of Jesus Christ. It's mind boggling to say the least. The church as we know it today in many aspects will soon be unrecognizable.

This book is a preparatory manual for every believer who is willing to make a successful transition into the 21st century. John Noble is a man ahead of his time who definitely has an insight into the new millennium. This is not ordinary or casual reading. This is a book only to be devoured by the Spirit person. It's truly radical reading from a radical British Christian leader and author. John Noble has been my friend since 1991. I feel John is truly a modern-day apostle with a heart for the world. He is a pioneer, foundation builder and father figure who is willing to set the pace for the next generation. He gives us all something to shoot for. I highly esteem this man of God and highly recommend these readings.

"The Shaking" is not just a book. It's an adventure.

Dale Gentry
Dale Gentry Ministries

INTRODUCTION

A major overhaul . . .

In 40 years of ministry my passion has been to see Jesus get the kind of church he deserves. A church which responds as a bride to her lover and as an army to its commander. Christine, my wife, says, "If you cut John he would bleed church."

However, I've been disappointed over the years that many Christians, particularly Charismatics, are concerned about their personal fulfilment and hardly troubled how Jesus feels. Leaders have tremendous ambitions for their church or network but little desire to co-operate to see Jesus honoured and his "great commission" completed.

There is little understanding among Protestants of our corporate destiny as the people of God, or the importance of unity across the streams. In our attempts to preserve the diversity which is our inheritance, we are more ready to divide than come together. Thus we diminish our testimony and our ability to achieve our objectives. In spite of this, the church worldwide is growing, which is down to God's grace, but don't be fooled. Powerful forces dedicated to stopping the advance of the gospel and reversing the growth are at work – materialism, false religion, globalization and persecution among them.

The church will never survive, let alone grasp the initiative to overcome, without a major overhaul. Thank God for yesterday's victories, but they were hindered by centuries of spiritual blindness and ignorance. Thankfully we are emerging from these dark ages through God's kindness in granting renewal, restoration and revival so we can meet the challenges of today and reach into every area of life.

... and a different kind of church

My colleague Martin Scott recently prophesied that it is time for Christians to identify the territory we believe God is giving us and come together to claim it through prayer and social involvement for the kingdom of God. "Together for territory" was his message.

Well, the ultimate "territory" is the world and the ultimate "togetherness" is the church. It is, indeed, time for the greatest forward thrust in our history and the banner we march under is love. Every street, village, town, people, group and nation must be given the life-bringing message of Jesus' love, over and over again.

For this we need a totally revamped church; a truly apostolic church moving in the example and power of Jesus, accessible, sensitive, flexible and alive with spiritual energy. A church less concerned with itself, its structures, meetings and buildings and more concerned about Jesus, our relationships and our task.

We must be seen to be a holy church, living out our values and beliefs in full view and open to scrutiny, challenging injustice and sin at the heart of this world and its systems. A church without walls. A fluid, moving church pouring itself out *among the people*, rather than unsuccessfully trying to persuade the people to pour themselves into *our* buildings, institutions and ghettos.

The Catholic view

I was extremely encouraged at a 2001 meeting of the ICCOWE[1] executive, now chaired by Charles Whitehead, well known in Catholic renewal. I'd been asked to speak on "what is the Spirit saying to the church?" along with Catholic theologian Father Peter Hocken. Our thoughts were not dissimilar although we had not consulted. Peter made three points which he expounded. They represent the heart of what this book is about:

Revelation – the Spirit is revealing the Father's heart concerning the fullness of his Son and the coming kingdom. The prophetic currents in the church must listen to God and one another!

Mobilization – the Spirit is mobilizing the whole body in worship, service, word, power and love. We must respond to his emphasis on reconciliation.

Transformation – the Spirit will take us beyond personal sanctification to communities transformed and creation redeemed.

The latter house?

So, the purpose of *The Shaking* is to help this fresh expression of church emerge. To enable ordinary Christians to understand the signs of the times and how God is at work among his people and the world in which they live. To help us recognize the new apostles who will encourage us to ponder God's question through the prophet, "Is it a time for you yourselves to be living in your panelled houses, while this [the Lord's] house remains a ruin?" (Haggai 1:4). To assure those who respond and fear the Lord that he is with us and "'the glory of this present house will be greater than the glory of the former house . . . and in this place I will grant peace,' declares the Lord Almighty" (2:9).

Every generation in touch with God must live as though it were the last. No generation has any other time or people it can directly influence but its own. However, if by faith and action we can make an impact now, that impact will continue should Jesus tarry.

Notes

1. International Charismatic Consultation on World Evangelization.

PART I

The preparation for change

CHAPTER 1

THE SHAKING!

"Once more I will shake not only the earth but also the heavens . . . so that what cannot be shaken may remain." (Hebrews 12:26–27).

An earthquake is a sudden release of energy in the earth's crust or upper mantle. As the planet's tectonic plates jostle against each other and become distorted, tremendous strain builds up – and from time to time the strain energy is discharged in zones where the rocks are weakest. The result is a sudden violent shock that can have highly destructive effects on the earth's surface nearby.

The Guinness Encyclopaedia.

Tangshan

At 3:42am on 27 July 1976 an earthquake struck Tangshan, a major industrial city of north-eastern China. Almost 800,000 men, women and children were wiped out, the vast majority crushed or trapped whilst asleep. Whole areas of soft sediment on which the city had been built liquefied, bringing down poorly constructed dwellings and multi-storey residential blocks. Special "quake-resistant" industrial buildings made of steel and concrete were razed to the ground in mangled heaps.

The devastation could not have been greater had a nuclear explosion taken place.

The initial shock, with a moment magnitude of 7.4, was followed by a 7.1 aftershock, when anything which withstood the first devastation was destroyed. But that was not the end of the suffering. Those who survived faced oppressive heat followed by flooding rain. Burst sewers and decomposing bodies polluted the water and diseases were rampant among the multitudes forced into makeshift open-air camps.

Panic seized other areas as millions fled their homes believing that shock waves could affect their towns and cities. In Beijing alone three-quarters of a million people took to the streets convinced it would be their turn next. Over 20 years have passed. Tangshan is rebuilt, but the terrors of that day remain etched in the minds of survivors who still tremble at the memory.

Genesis shaking

This most horrific earthquake was dwarfed by what happened in Noah's day. Then the heavens opened, releasing an incredible deluge for 40 days, which drained the heavens. "Fountains of the deep," vast underground seas, under colossal pressure, thrust upwards to meet the torrent. All life was utterly destroyed. Only Noah, his family and a handful of animals emerged into a totally reshaped world. Here God's rainbow of promise heralded a new age of blessing to come when the ark of Jesus' body would carry not animals of every kind, but people from every nation, tribe and tongue to a new heaven and earth, purged, not by water, but by the Spirit's refining fire.

The shaking continues . . .

The Lord will never again destroy the earth by flood, but his promise, "Once more I will shake . . ." remains. Shakings,

mighty rushing winds and tongues of fire will persist until creation is cleansed of all that is injurious and ungodly. That is
apparent when he says, "Not only the earth but also the heavens
will be shaken." The careful observer of events in the church
and around the world will recognize the beginnings of shaking
which will continue until heaven, earth and hell yield to God's
unwavering purpose "to bring all things . . . together under one
head, even Christ" (Ephesians 1:10).

Speaking of the Greek world view which separates heaven
from earth, Jim Thwaites in *The Church Beyond the
Congregation* (Paternoster Press), says:

> We have inherited philosophical terrain with a great fault line
> running through it. It is now coming under intense and increasing
> pressure. This is the real estate that we here sold to the saints. This
> is the terrain that they in turn have built their homes and lives upon.
> The tectonic plates are shifting, the cracks are visible and the time
> of reckoning is now.

Every throne, principality, power and authority, whether
human or angelic, not ordained by God, will fall. "The
Shaking" will identify tremors sending out their warning
signals and discerning saints will prayerfully prepare themselves, their families and their churches for what is going to be
the most far-reaching shakedown in history. Nothing will
escape the scrutiny of the Divine Quality Controller. Pure gold
alone will gain the hallmark of his approval.

Everything built on the rock of Jesus Christ will stand. Man-
made and demon-inspired structures will be blown away. Every
religious activity or church programme not rooted in Christ's
love and sustained by the Spirit will go. Finally, the world
system, motivated by greed, resourced by money and controlled by devils, will fail in one hour! The collapse of communism was a sign, a prophetic precursor of what's to come. One

day it was there, a vast, apparently invincible empire – the next
it was gone.

> Woe! Woe, O great city,
> O Babylon, city of power!
> In one hour your doom has come!
>   (Revelation 18:10)

"I will build . . ."

Concerning the church, Jesus was clear from the start – "I will
build my church; and the gates of hell shall not prevail against
it" (Matthew 16:18, AV). His words are comforting and chilling.
Comforting because hell must give up its captives, chilling
because any building work not ordered by Jesus will fall,
however impressive.

We Christians have an inherent belief that our churches are
invincible. Ancient mission halls, from whence the Spirit has
long since gone and where even non-Christians see "Ichabod"
– "the glory has departed" (1 Samuel 4:21) – written over their
doors, are kept open as a "witness." How can a bickering dozen
saints in a dilapidated hall where years ago the treasurer ran off
with the choir mistress be a witness? In Revelation 2:5 even the
great Ephesian church was warned, "If you do not repent, I will
come to you and remove your lampstand." For lampstand read
witness or church!

Nor will our streams and denominations escape God's scrutiny; all must be tested by earthquake, wind and holy fire.
History is peppered with men who have grasped the initiative for
building church from Jesus by relying on their own resources.
The bareness of much that exists today is a solemn reminder to
avoid such arrogance and sectarianism. Those days are past.
Let's hand back the control to Jesus – the only one equipped to
lead us into an effective, world-changing future together.

Of course, the Christian record is not all bad. Later we will remind ourselves how God has worked through the lives of faithful women and men who, like Jesus, were marginalized, maligned and martyred by those who claimed to lead his church.

Times of refreshing

Today millions of Christians all over the world are fasting and interceding for a fresh, powerful move of God. In Acts 3:19, Peter promises if we repent, our sins will be forgiven and times of refreshing will come from the Lord. Repentance means a change of heart and attitude, and giving up our rights to determine our own future. It means allowing the Lord freedom to develop the church as he chooses. It means letting go of the past, even blessings, to embrace a new understanding of church as God intends it.

It stands to reason things must change. If the Western church of the last 50 years has failed to impact society for good, it will not do so in the next 50 unless there are major shifts in understanding and practice. Get ready! The Lord is committed, through discipline and judgement, to show that the church is his chosen people, his royal priesthood, his holy nation (1 Peter 2:9).

Generations together

Every generation which experiences an outpouring of revival resists the next. Criticism, pride, rejection and even persecution have been the norm. This is tragic, for those who have responded to the Spirit have no mentors or spiritual mothers and fathers. Extremes abound, fuelling the fires of those who would condemn the new movement.

The spiritual tempo is quickening. There is no time for a

process of reaction, repentance and repairing relationships. The generations must find grace to work together. Jeff Lucas, a vice president of the Evangelical Alliance in the UK, gives us the equation for success: adolescent diversity alone = rebellion; mature unity alone = repression, but adolescent diversity + mature unity = release!

The "Abrahams," fathers in the church, must continue to work with second generation "Isaacs" who've served faithfully in their father's house. Then the "Abrahams" and "Isaacs" must adapt, without compromising their values, to accommodate the third generation "Jacobs." This generation needs real encouragement to find its identity without spending unnecessary years in isolation.

To use another analogy, "Joshua" and "Caleb" will cross the Jordan with the new generation and wrest the promised land from the grip of our enemy. Now is the time. We hear the rumblings as the Holy Spirit moves, breaking down our resistance and challenging our preconceptions. More and more saints, tired of lukewarm, powerless Christianity, are groaning, bowing down and crying out, "Yes, Lord!"

Better throw ourselves on God's mercy, trusting our churches to his judgement, rather than fashion our own destiny or, worse, fall into the hands of our enemy. It's a real battle; there will be casualties; we will face demolition before we see building, but God is good and has a vested interest in the church for his Son's sake. His only Son, who loved the church and sacrificed himself to make her holy ". . . without stain or wrinkle or any other blemish" (Ephesians 5:26–27). Let's put our lives in his hands so he can radically reshape us and turn us inside out so we can turn the world upside down!

CHAPTER 2

ARMAGEDDON NOW!

The end is nigh

An object is hurtling towards us. Our planet faces extinction. Its people are under sentence of death, and we are right to be afraid. Worse, it's not a meteorite we can destroy with a nuclear device. The approaching danger is invisible, more fearsome. Absolutely nothing can be done to stop it. Its arrival is inevitable, as certain as the rising sun. Some call it "Armageddon," "The Final Battle." I call it – "The Future"!

With a new millennium awareness of impending doom increases. "The Future" looms and the need for a messiah to deliver us is more evident each day. Science fiction and movies feed our imaginations with external threats of aliens and evil forces, but it is the demon within we should fear. Time is running out for the human race.

Deceived by the "god of this world" into believing we can be masters of our future, politicians, scientists and wealth-creators juggle, not simply with atoms, but with DNA, the substance of life itself. So, playing God with creation for power and personal gain, they seek the elixir of eternal life. Ignoring Christ's command to "seek first his kingdom and righteousness" these people lust after material things which our heavenly Father will add to us anyway. Jesus showed us the way to obtain real power by opening the door for us to become sons of God, and inheritors of all things good.

Jesus redeemed power and declared, "all authority in heaven and on earth has been given to me, therefore go . . ." (Matthew 28:18–19). He urges us to go as disciples in the same Spirit of humility and power. God's promises are clear: "it is your Father's good pleasure to give you the kingdom" (Luke 12:32, AV); "the meek . . . shall inherit the earth" (Matthew 5:5, AV); "God . . . richly provides us with everything for our enjoyment" (1 Timothy 6:17). What more could we ask? But the Lord resists the proud, and the humble receive grace.

World trends

Dr Patrick Dixon is founder of the international AIDS agency ACET and director of Global Change Ltd. His website – www.globalchange.com – received 4.5 million hits in 12 months. Some time ago Patrick took the word F-U-T-U-R-E as an acrostic to focus on world trends, and has used this in lectures alerting business people, politicians and major financial institutions to the enormous shifts taking place in society. These trends run parallel but at times are in violent conflict as the world adjusts to massive growth in population and knowledge, and to the divisions between the "haves" and the "have nots." His book *Futurewise* (HarperCollins) covers the trends in detail. Here I've used his headings and my additions to help us make sense of the shakings taking place in our world.

F = FAST

More change has taken place in our lifetime than in the rest of history. In the past 40 years world trade has increased by

1,500%. The pace is accelerating daily as miniaturization and technological development put the impossible within our reach. China alone reported an increase of 400% in Internet users in 1997. Within a few years we will be able to download almost any piece of literature that was ever written.

Information is the new currency. An injectable chip is already here with a memory, transmitter and receiver. It needs no batteries and will last 100 years. Planted under the skin of the wrist or forehead it could eliminate the need for cash, and speed travel, shopping and criminal investigation. Increasingly the world's wealth is in the hands of fewer people. This rich elite will commandeer the last remnants of our vanishing countryside. From these safe havens they will conduct business through TV and telephone links with all corners of the globe.

U = URBAN

Whilst the rich escape to their garden paradise the poor will languish in hell city. Now around 80% of the world's population lives in cities. For decades people from rural areas in all parts of the world have been pouring into cities in search of food and work. Not long ago Greater London, with its 12 million inhabitants, was one of the largest cities in the world. Today it is not even in the top ten. The resulting problems are obvious: poverty, slums, disease, crime, prostitution, abandoned children . . .

The first city built by the murderer Cain, in the land of Nod (meaning "restless") is the foundation of today's cities. Like Abraham our father, we look for another city, whose maker and builder is God (Hebrews 11:10). A new Jerusalem, meaning "possession of peace," coming from out of heaven to earth (Revelation 21:2).

T = TRIBAL

The marginalization of groups and sub-cultures within society produces a crisis of identity. The need to be recognized, and have land you can call home, is producing violent reactions. On one hand hooliganism invades the football terraces, on the other ethnic strife involves exterminating millions of innocent souls. Northern Ireland, Kosovo, Sudan, the Middle East, Rwanda, are just some of the civil war-torn areas of recent years. The whole earth is boiling with unrest.

Headlines announce the plight of refugees herded into make-shift camps as displaced people flee their oppressors. Human rights activists lobby governments and the UN seeking justice and resources for these sorry masses. Beyond obvious needs of food, medicine and shelter lies the deeper need to regain a lost identity. The robbery of a people's soul, the imposition of one culture upon another, is deeply wounding. Should the pains of war be healed, the soul-numbing question of identity remains.

U = UNIVERSAL

Huge multinational companies, banks and consortiums, greedy for new markets, are producing a frightening uniformity every-where. Ecological, health, financial, political and policing prob-lems are just a few of the difficulties which demand global answers. National and local governments have no means to handle such complexities. World government is inevitable, and we need it. The question is, who rules?

Little-reported major New Age and environmental confer-ences discuss these issues with popular personalities and world leaders. A strategy for world peace and conservation based on Luciferic principles (see chapter 3) is being prepared and Russia's ex-president Gorbachev,[1] through his "State of the World Forum," has an important role. Apparently he is being schooled as the first leader of the New World Order. Professor

Henry Lamb of The University of Texas in a paper, "The Rise of Global Governance," documents the history and links of this New Age movement with the UN in its many parts. At the time of writing, this paper was available on the University website – www.utexas.edu/.

Richard Yan, one of a new breed of Chinese entrepreneurs, said in *Time* Magazine, "You can't stop globalization. Information and knowledge are the biggest equalizers in the world. Bottom line, I really believe the world will become one."

R = RADICAL

To quote Patrick Dixon, "the future will have a strong radical element to it, as traditional political movements shrivel and die." News-hungry media provide endless opportunities for the angry agitator and terrorist alike. Freedom fighters, suicide bombers, religious fanatics, ecological protesters and political sleaze-hunters can grab international attention and hold a government, a nation, to ransom. Single-issue politics will increasingly determine the outcome of elections, or an individual nation may play super-powers off one against the other. Remember Cuba, Iraq and Libya?

We might say that with a free press such opportunities may be grasped by the weak to bring their cries for justice to the attention of the world. Sadly this is not the case, since peaceful demonstration is not newsworthy. Furthermore, the news is selective and biased towards the privileged and the violent. The largest prayer meeting in history, when 12 million people "Marched for Jesus", was ignored, but a couple of terrorists taking hostages will fill our screens for days.

E = ETHICAL

Genetic engineering, abortion, euthanasia, international debt, slave labour, are some of the issues crying out for an international code of ethics. As God is dead and we have abandoned moral absolutes, who decides right from wrong? Today one of the most dangerous places in the world for a baby is its mother's womb! According to *Hansard*[2] there were almost 4.7 million abortions in the UK in the 30 years between 1967, when the act was brought in, and 31 March 1997. Furthermore, William Wilberforce, campaigner against slavery, would turn in his grave if he realized that 150 years on, whole nations would be enslaved in chains of debt.

At the time of Moses' birth, and also when Jesus was born, the fear of a promised deliverer caused the wholesale slaughter of male children. Perhaps today, because we are about to witness the birth of a deliverer generation who will publish the good news far and wide, Satan has sought to annihilate them through abortion? It seems he did this in 1910 when Christians, involved in missions across the world, came together at the "Edinburgh Conference" to plan a major thrust in global evangelization. Then we were plunged into successive world wars which stopped their efforts and all but wiped the missionary force out completely.

The burning question

The "F-U-T-U-R-E" is upon us. Armageddon approaches – this generation or the next . . . ? We can't be sure but the conclusion of history cannot be changed; there must be a final confrontation between good and evil, and we've read the last chapter of the book. The question we must ask ourselves, our churches, our Christian organizations is this – what are we living for and for what are we prepared to die?

It will not be our institutions, buildings or forms of worship that will hold our allegiance. Few would lay down their lives for these. No, when everything superfluous is stripped away, what remains will be the basic minimum without which we cannot exist – our relationship with Jesus, our love for one another and our determination to see his kingdom come. This is the essence of the cross which he calls us to carry through this world of broken promises and shattered dreams.

The road to destruction

"While people are saying, 'Peace and safety', destruction will come on them suddenly . . ." (1 Thessalonians 5:3). When we become preoccupied with ourselves and leave God out of the equation, that which looks good can turn sour very quickly. History confirms this and warns us that the future is bound to be full of surprises.

One world

In Europe today people are divided over the mixed blessings of unity. The British are hesitant to adopt the European currency and the Germans have a strong anti-European feeling. Norway has long expressed fears about joining the community and is keenly independent. Tribal instincts thrive in all of our countries. Nevertheless, the dilemma which faces us does not concern involvement in a European community but the pressing need to be part of a common world market and community. As I said, the problems confronting governments today can't be handled locally. They're of global significance and demand universal co-operation.

Never has the need been so urgent, or the world so obviously prepared for the arrival of a saviour. Democracy as we know it is all but dead. Western governments maintain a semblance of control, tinkering with local issues of tax, employment, health and education, but the power base has quietly shifted. We have no option but to unite together behind an authority which can address the real issues that confront us all.

POLLUTION

It's not the mountains of waste or untreated sewage thrown up on our beaches that are the main problems. Nor is it CFC gas blowing holes in the ozone layer, or nuclear waste dumped in our oceans or buried where our families live that's the primary concern. It's not about acid rain, exhaust fumes or the destruction of rainforest, nor even global warming producing freak floods and famine. Vital though it will be for an international body to deal with these things, this is the devil we know. What of the devil we do not know?

Individuals or groups with purpose, who suddenly find unbelievable power in their hands, are the unknown quantity, the pollution in society itself. Teenagers who gun down fellow pupils in school; the fanatic brandishing a tiny phial of lethal bactcria over a nation's water supply; or the mini-dictator with nerve gas which could wipe out one third of the world's population. Are these the horsemen of the apocalypse, riding forth with destruction in their wake?

The AIDS virus may not have been a political conspiracy to control population, but it is entirely possible that some mad scientist will give his Hitler the means to manipulate the world. Hollywood doom fantasies touch a nerve in our psyche, but they immunize us against the awful reality. It really could happen. Someone must come and save us – a new messiah?

POPULATION

Population is fast becoming a pollutant. There is only so much land to farm, air to breathe and oil to burn, and supplies are dwindling. We may abhor China's one child per family policy which has produced unwanted girl babies and the horror of the "dying rooms," but something must be done.

David Barrett's "Annual Statistical Table on Global Missions 1994" made a mind-numbing observation. "Consider the UN's projected world population for AD 2150. The most frightening scenario, based on human fertility continuing throughout 1990–2150 at the same level as today (4.3 children per woman), foresees a world population in 2150 of 694 billion, a population density 122 times today's." Our world cannot sustain that kind of growth. To some, euthanasia, abortion and the selective culling of the sick and deformed are not such awful propositions. Who will help us take the terrible decisions needed to halt population explosion?

MONEY

Amschel Mayer (later Baron Rothschild), who funded Britain and the continent during the Napoleonic War, and whose family headed up the International Banking Syndicate, allegedly said, "I care not who rules a nation, he who hold the purse strings has the power." Jesus made it crystal clear, the choice is God or money (Matthew 6:24). Money itself is not evil, but to be obsessed with wealth is the ultimate deception. Riches provide ultimate power and therefore corrupt absolutely.

In his temptation the devil promised Jesus the kingdoms of this world if he bowed in worship. Jesus rejected the proposition and chose the cross as his way to power. The offer stands, but this way to power is anti-Christ and this spirit is all around us. The world's wealth is in the hands of fewer people, making it easier to control.

Today money rules. $1.3 trillion are traded every day! During the monetary crisis in Britain under John Major's government the Bank of England bolstered UK currency with a £10 billion ($15 billion US) injection. According to reports at the time, five major consortiums poured £150 billion ($225 billion US) into the markets to tip the balance the other way. There is a hidden body who, through buying and selling commodities and arms (to all sides in a conflict) and by manipulating currencies, controls much of the world's wealth and therefore control the world. Will such people provide our deliverer?

Scripture is clear: "the love of money is a root of all kinds of evil" (1 Timothy 6:10). Jesus' teaching concerning God and money, and the general tenor of the Bible supports this statement. Such references as Psalm 26:5 to the "assembly of evildoers," Revelation 2:9 & 3:9 to "a synagogue of Satan" point to the devil as highly intelligent and organized with a strategy worked out through dedicated people – his church, his body on earth. The temporary rewards are "the kingdoms of the world."

CRIME

Crime and money are linked, although criminals are the visible and less dangerous tip of the wealth iceberg. We in the West despise the open corruption of many poorer nations, but in all countries, despite the cloak of respectability, the criminal network thrives not far underground. Protection rackets, slave prostitution, drug barons, tax fraudsters, paedophile rings, secret societies and Mafia enclaves abound.

In *The Changing Shape of World Mission* Bryant Myers tells us that organized crime costs the world $600 billion a year, drug traffic $150 billion, financial crime $2,000 billion, fraud $500 billion. The total cost of these "structures of sin" is $5.2 trillion every year! Furthermore, Myers points out that it would take a mere $520 billion annually to provide the world's poor with food, water, education and shelter!

Attempts have been made to defeat the public aspects of these criminal networks, but they simply become more sophisticated, or relocate. There is growing co-operation amongst the police internationally, but even here there are reports of corruption, sometimes at the highest levels. The press is at last questioning the numbers of freemasons in the police and judicial system, and in the USA the FBI are constantly under scrutiny for cover-ups and conspiracies. Understandably the investigative process requires data to succeed in the fight against crime, but is the need for information an infringement of our freedom? Is "big brother's" eye on anyone who bucks the system?

Already in many parts of the world churches not recognized by the state are labelled as cults and their members seen as potential trouble makers. This is not fantasy. The wheels are turning this way in Europe and, in addition to Muslim nations where one would expect it, Russia, Israel, and others are well down the road of discrimination against Christians. It would be a strange irony if the resources amassed to beat the criminal were used against the people of God whose only desire is to do good.

NATIONALISM

Ethnic strife is bubbling up in every place. Old wounds, which we thought were long since healed, open up again amongst peoples previously controlled by communism. In the UK, with no threat of war to draw us together, the pace of devolution quickens as the nations of the union claim more independence. This is understandable when we consider our history and the pain we have inflicted on one another.

Arguments continue as to whether the good achieved through the British Empire outweighs the bad. However, some of those who formerly lived under British rule tell us that the corruption of their own systems is greater than anything experienced during British colonial administration. This does not excuse our past sins nor the need to seek forgiveness, but confirms we must all scrutinize our own backyard. I was with an American family on one of my visits and was sharing how ashamed I was about some of our British past. The son, a fine

Christian teenager, was amazed. He said that he believed the big mistake the early settlers made in his country was their failure to completely eradicate the native Americans!

The arrogance of the English in our treatment of the Irish, Scots and Welsh has been contemptible. Our inhumanity in refusing to alleviate suffering during the potato famine in Ireland, clearances which dispossessed thousands in the Highlands of Scotland and the rape of resources with the imposition of our culture in Wales, all contributed to the anger still evident. But few are without guilt in these matters.

Church empowered in weakness

Throughout history, racial pride coupled with militarism which focuses on land, has accounted for the slaughter of untold millions. However, the "might is right" approach inevitably leads to those who live by the sword also dying by the sword. The great empires have largely disappeared or will soon give way to the super-power.

With communism outside China largely defunct and China struggling, Islam and Christianity may soon remain alone to challenge secular humanism and all-consuming materialism. Mind you, Islam is under threat from globalization and the New World Order, and it will not happily flow into a religious masala. So will it survive? Maybe the more pertinent question is – will Christianity survive? The powerful link in Britain and parts of Europe between politics and institutional Christianity is already being severely tested. If separation comes between church and state (as of course applies in the USA and elsewhere), soon the church's spiritual authority may be all that remains to buck the system.

This weakening of the church will be her salvation. Stripped of worldly power and increasingly endowed with power from on high, she will be the primary opposition to the Luciferic throne of the rising new Satanic age. That throne is referred to in Revelation 2:13 and the "deep secrets" of Satan in 2:24. Today it is uncovered at the heart of "New Age" and is central to establishing an all-embracing world faith. This has been well documented in many Christian books (e.g. *What is the New Age?* by Cole, Graham, Hyton and Lewis [Hodder and Stoughton]). I quote from Basilea Schlink's pamphlet *New Age from a Biblical Viewpoint*:

> David Spangler, a prominent New Age leader and for three years co-director of the Findhorn Foundation . . . wrote . . . in one of his numerous books: "Lucifer works within each of us to bring us to wholeness, and as we move into a new age, which is the age of man's wholeness, each of us in some way is brought to that point which I term the Luciferic initiation (an act of consecration to Lucifer), the particular doorway through which the individual must pass if he is to come fully into the presence of his light and his wholeness."(D. Sprangler – 'Reflections on the Christ' as quoted by Cumby, op. cit., p.139).
>
> Spangler, who frequently made contact with the demonic world, publicly explained that the true light of Findhorn was the light of Lucifer, who is to illumine the world.
>
> At the core of the planned New World Religion is the initiation (act of consecration), openly termed as "Luciferic" not only by David Spangler but previously by Helena Blavatsky and Alice Bailey in their writings. Various leaders of the Movement have attempted to deify Lucifer. According to Alice Bailey, Lucifer is the "Ruler of Humanity". In any event he is the guiding light of today's New Age Movement.

However, not everything going on in the world is evil. The Holy Spirit is also at work, and we need the gift of discernment (1 Corinthians 12:10) to differentiate. As the Lord recognized and faced demonic opposition with confidence, so will his people.

His words, "'whatever you bind on earth will be bound in heaven, and whatever you loose on earth will be loosed in heaven'" (Matthew 16:19 & 18:18[3]) are assurance that the keys of death and hell have been placed in our hands.

The picture in Revelation 22 assures us that the righteous are like trees planted by water. Rooted in our relationship with Christ, we draw from the river of the Holy Spirit which flows from God's throne – the source of our life and power. We will be known by our fruits and the leaves will be medicine to bring healing to the nations.

Notes

1. One or two friends have advised me that these comments and those on pages 242–243 under "Moving the goalposts" should be removed, as they suggest a conspiracy, and this could undermine the credibility of this book and weaken my other arguments in the minds of many sincere Christians. However, my conviction in the light of the evidence mentioned here and elsewhere, is such that I feel it important to raise an alarm. Satan is an intelligent being, created by God and, in my opinion is working systematically through history, people and institutions to achieve his ends. I pray that more Christians with the capacity to do so will research these matters. If I am proved to be wrong nothing is lost but my reputation, in which case please forgive me. If I am right then we will be more prepared to face the future together.
2. Hansard is the official record of debates in the UK's Parliament.
3. See Appendix 1 and pages 152 and 155.

CHAPTER 3

EARTHQUAKE, WIND AND FIRE

The Lord said, "Go out and stand on the mountain in the presence of the Lord, for the Lord is about to pass by" (1 Kings 19:11).

Earthquake, wind and fire, symbols of God's judgement, are to be feared. For Christians, however, discipline, although painful, is to be welcomed. It is a sign of his love, evidence that we're his children (Hebrews 12:5–6, see also chapter 13). Such is his care for us he is unwilling to allow us to remain in immaturity, destroying one another with petty, childish ways. He is committed to make us holy as he is holy, so that through obedience we may enter the joys and privileges of sonship. Our difficulties arise when we fail to understand what God is doing and why.

Elijah experienced God's power in amazing ways. His story is found in 1 Kings 17 through to 2 Kings 2. Although he was a great man of God and exercised great faith, he too had weaknesses and needed God's discipline. The Lord raised him up to challenge king Ahab, who led Israel into all kinds of evil. In the midst of bringing God's judgement of drought to the king and his people, he experienced testing and was shaken to the core.

In the same way many Christians and churches are being unexpectedly shaken today.

Learning from Elijah's story

As we pick up his story, Elijah was experiencing a high – perhaps too high! The prophets of Baal had failed miserably to persuade their god to prove himself by sending fire. Elijah's mocking sent them into a frenzy of self-flagellation, cutting their flesh. "Maybe your God's on vacation or gone to the toilet!" he taunts. With unswerving faith he builds his altar, slays his beast and pours water (a rare commodity in view of the drought) on the sacrifice, again and again.

The fire falls; Baal's prophets tremble; the crowd's aghast. After the roar of flames, an eerie silence, then screams of approval, – "Eli-jah! Eli-jah!" "God is God! God is God!" The chant goes on. Do they honour the Lord or is Elijah their hero? The blood flows in rivulets down Carmel as God's man drives home his victory. Four hundred and fifty prophets of Baal perish, yet evil Jezebel remains unscathed. Now for rain!

"The prayer of a righteous man is powerful and effective", says James 5:16. Elijah prayed for rain, and it came in torrents. Despite no sign of rain it came as a deluge. The prophet's high became a roll, the enemy was on the run, only a woman stood in the way. Jezebel was wicked Ahab's wife, the power behind the throne, urging her husband into idolatry and depravity and goading the man of God. Elijah's faith has been an inspiration over centuries, but the Bible not only records success but also failure, and there's much to be learned from both.

Most vulnerable in success

Jezebel's threat sends Elijah into a spin. For the first time he journeys without a directive from God. He runs; self-doubt and depression follow and suicidal thoughts are not far behind. In Horeb's cave he rests, with hopes of meeting the Lord as Moses had here before him. God has not deserted him; there is more for him to do, but still faith and obedience are required – without them it's impossible to please him.

"What are you doing here, Elijah?" The Lord's question is fair; he has not sent him there. Self-pity blinded the prophet, yet he is not alone. Seven thousand others remain faithful in those dark days. The Lord is gracious; he has come to the place of Elijah's need to reveal himself. "Go out and stand on the mountain . . . for the Lord is about to pass by." Still Elijah refrains, gripped by pain and frustration. Wind blows, earthquake shakes and fire burns, but not until the gentle whisper does he go to the mouth of the cave. Still the pain prevails: "God, don't you care I'm alone?"

How often our feelings hinder us from grasping what God says. Self-preoccupation will keep us from understanding the full significance of God's commission. How would Israel have fared had Elijah immediately obeyed and done all that he was commanded? Four things were required; only two were done. Thus Israel endured more hard years under Ahab's family.

Let's not be quick to pass judgement on the man of God. It was he, together with Moses, who appeared on the mount when Jesus was transfigured (Matthew 17:3). These two witnesses of the old Law and prophets stood with Peter, James and John, first fruits of a new order of the Spirit, with Jesus the bridge. However, like Moses and all God's people, Elijah was human. He was one of us and most vulnerable in success.

The Toronto lesson

Since the outpouring of the Holy Spirit in renewal on the Airport Vineyard church in Toronto, tens of thousands of

Christians worldwide have been blessed and lives have been radically changed. In Britain thousands of churches were shaken as the wind of God swept through whole congregations. Trust, built up over years among leaders across streams and denominations, provided a network of relationships that God could use. The descriptions of what took place compare with other seasons when God visited his people and all the analogies of wind, earthquakes and fire have been used.

In Holy Trinity Brompton, an Anglican church in central London, a newspaper reporter told how she actually felt wind as she sat recording what was taking place. Others described the Spirit's coming as a mighty wind bending and breaking the people. In Pioneer, leaders have testified to powerful shakings: thrilling and chilling at the same time. Sadly, some resisted, finding the challenge too great, but mostly we saints are more open, more prayerful and more ready for whatever God has than at any previous time.

References to fire regularly appear in conference literature and book titles. Stories from people who tell how they have been purified in God's refining flames and set ablaze with his love are commonplace. All this is wonderful, but as the intensity subsides and the phenomena become an accepted part of our lives, a deep questioning remains. What *is* God saying in all this?

Exhilarating laughter, heartrending tears, joyful reconciliation, groans, animal noises which, incidentally, are not without biblical support, (Micah 1:8 etc), and bodies strewn on the floor . . . "Thank you, Lord!" But where is it leading? The lost world is largely unmoved and it's business as usual. The unreached are yet unreached, the sick remain unwell, the oppressed are still oppressed and the rich get richer. Cynics deride, optimists exaggerate, pessimists undervalue what God's done and pragmatists go back to doing whatever has to be done. But God hasn't finished with us yet.

Caution: Holy Spirit at work!

Dr Michael Moynagh in *Changing World Changing Church* (Monarch Books), argues that the church's mission is bigger than evangelism. He says we're called to "bring society closer to God's values" and "the church's central task is not to colonize society for God, but to attend to what God is already doing in the world." John Drane, *The McDonaldization of the Church* (Darton, Longman and Todd), says, "Mission for me . . . becomes a matter of recognizing what God is already doing (the *Missio Dei*), and getting alongside that . . ."

Something is happening. The Holy Spirit is at work out there. During Easter 2001 the *Daily Telegraph* reported that 30% of people who were asked if they believed in the bodily resurrection of Jesus said "Yes!" It may not take a great deal to convert people from believing *about* Jesus to believing *in* Jesus. A quiet revival could take place very quickly and some Christians might not even notice. After Princess Diana's death an amazing prophecy came to light which had been given in the May before her accident in August 1997. It spoke of a nation in mourning, putting flowers in the cities, and went on ". . . my Spirit will be moving faster than those flowers are removed."

No one could have foreseen it would take six weeks to remove flowers. That's a long time to remove a few flowers, but it's a short time to change the heart of a nation! Some felt revival would come after the flowers had gone. For my part, I believe God was simply saying that's how quickly my Spirit *can* move, and I await the day with expectancy.

Get out of the cave

Are we so preoccupied with ourselves that we cannot hear what God has said? "Get out of your cave, Elijah! Stop hiding; go and stand on the mountain, for I will pass by!" God works at his own pace and in his own way; he will not alter course or change plans to accommodate our emotional lows or highs, even though he loves us.

His explanation may not have been in the wind, earthquake or fire, or in trembling bodies or laughter, but they are all part of God's shaping process. He is preparing us for involvement in the next great phase of human history. Elijah means "God is God." He must do his work to awaken hearts and make way for Elisha – "God is Saviour." As John made way for Jesus, so we, his church, must do the same today.

Through renewal, the Lord's alerted us to his coming. The shaking tells us he is on the move. It's an advance warning of his intention to retrieve his church from self-seekers and kingdom-builders. God will be God to his people, so he can be Saviour to the world. As we wait patiently with eyes turned to Jesus, we shall be changed. Wind, earthquake and fire will prepare us to hear and obey the still small voice when it comes. Stop hiding, get out of the cave, stand on the mountain; the Lord is about to pass by!

If we yield, God's dealings will transform us. The process may be slow, even painful, but God is committed. He will not leave us as we are, but will change us from "one degree of his glory to another" until we appear like him in holiness, love and power. This is the church Jesus deserves and this is the church he will have: a church which does not seek after signs or trivialize them, nor fear or dismiss them, but patiently endeavours to see the direction they are pointing. Shakings, wind and fire will be followed by the still small voice if we wait. God's shaking is to a purpose.

CHAPTER 4

HISTORY-MAKERS

Is it true today that when people pray
Cloudless skies will break,
Kings and queens will shake?
Yes it's true and I believe it,
I'm living for you.

I'm gonna be a history-maker in this land.
I'm gonna be a speaker of truth to all mankind.
I'm gonna stand, I'm gonna run
Into your arms, into your arms again:
Into your arms, into your arms again.

Is it true today that when people pray
We'll see dead men rise
And the blind set free?
Yes it's true and I believe it,
I'm living for you.

Yes it's true today that when people stand
With the fire of God, with the truth in hand,
We'll see miracles, we'll see angels sing,
We'll see broken hearts making history.
Yes it's true and we believe it,
We're living for you.

Martin Smith © 1996 Curious? Music UK,
by kind permission of Furious? Records

Before we can face the challenges ahead, we must be brutally honest. The history of the church shows that it is possible for revival to come and go without making any lasting change. Not that we're good at measuring. I wonder what effect the widow's mite will have had when these matters are judged? One simple act had such profound consequences, when we seem to expend so much energy to achieve so little! More time spent asking God what he requires might help put us alongside the history-makers. As Martin Smith puts it – "We're living for you!"

Gerald Coates, co-founder of "March for Jesus" has been my friend for years. I've admired Gerald's prophetic ability to look beyond the obvious to challenge the status quo. When renewal began its shaking in May 1994, Gerald stepped back from all that was happening. He wanted to understand what the Lord was seeking to communicate beyond the obvious blessing of encouragement. He came with a clear word which did not hinder our receiving, but helped us remain focused for the long haul.

He reminded us that when the Holy Spirit fell at Pentecost, two questions were asked – "What does this mean?" (Acts 2:12) and "What shall we do?" (Acts 2:37). Understanding the signs and knowing how to react are imperative if we are to avoid missing God's purpose. Jesus urges us to read the signs and to understand the times we live in. His tragic judgement on Jerusalem, as he wept over the city, was given because the people didn't recognize the hour of their visitation (Luke 19:44). They missed their opportunity to become history-makers.

Welsh revival or tragedy?

The Welsh revival of 1904 is an example of an outpouring of the wine of God's blessing with no wineskins to preserve it.

Lives were changed. One hundred thousand people were converted to Christ in three years. Communities were turned upside down and shock waves were felt around the world. However, the critics prevailed and the revival fires subsided.

The conversions mostly stood the test of time. Many gave themselves in missionary service but were lost on battlefields in World War I. Within a generation legalism prevailed and genuine worship quickly turned to nostalgia. No one recognized the need to adjust the structures, practices and the shape of the church. The grace which had touched so many should have translated into joyful, holy living and passed on to their children. In that way the history of Wales would have been changed forever.

It's relatively easy to make sacrifices in the midst of an outpouring of God's blessing. Many did in Wales and we, too, must be willing to lay aside even legitimate things when God calls. However, was sacrifice what God wanted, or was it obedience? Obedience can be more demanding.

Learning to live in moderation can be as important a spiritual exercise as abstinence. Paul learned how to handle abundance and to suffer deprivation (Philippians 4:12). In our culture "abundance" may mean material resources or the opportunity to enjoy the cinema, sport, drink and dancing. Of course these can be obstacles to going on with God, but to deny one another these things in the name of holiness, as happened in Wales, is to misunderstand the nature of grace. In this way we can actually close the door to God's mercy and open ourselves to pride through legalistic works.

So Wales became hardened to the gospel and resistant to the Holy Spirit. It is significant that after four decades of renewal, there is no Welsh-speaking charismatic church.

In *The Church Beyond the Congregation*, Jim Thwaites makes the point:

Revivals carry people along in their fervour like a mighty wave, with a power hard to resist. It is after the revival moves on that the time comes for the saints to build a life with the truth given to them . . . Revival does not of itself usher in the long-term restoration of the city or region.

Gerald Coates says, "Revival is not what we want, it is what we need to get what we want – society leavened with the Kingdom of God."

In Israel, when the tribes were living in harmony as God intended, there were no divisions between sacred and secular. All of life was holy. Worship, work, enjoyment were blended together in a symphony with God the conductor. For grace not only saves us but, like sweet perfume, it also pervades every aspect of life. The church today must fling open every window and door. No dark, stuffy or unkempt rooms for us: Jesus must be welcome everywhere.

God can do it again

God has not deserted Wales, and the Spirit is stirring again. Among many others my wife, Christine, smitten with a concern for Wales, began to network with churches and Christian leaders. The hunger to see God move is growing and old wells of God's blessing have been revisited with tears of repentance, crying for God to intervene.

There is an openness to pray together. Streams of creativity are beginning to flow as Christians become involved in the arts, reaching out to the poor and the youth sub-culture in their language and music. Some churches are growing and hope is breaking out like spring flowers. Prophesies concerning wildfire falling in Wales and arching through England into Europe have helped ignite prayer. May it be so, Lord!

As we strive to understand what God is saying through renewal and seek to determine what we should do, we must consider the bigger picture. We must get out of the confines of our "cave" and stand on the "mountain," where we can see more clearly. We must forsake introversion and leave behind parochialism as well as tribal loyalties and national pride. Yes, God loves me and my church, he cares about my stream and the country I belong to, but all these must be held in the light of what he is doing across time and in the whole earth.

History or history-makers?

If we are history-makers and not merely pawns in the game of life, we will see things from God's perspective. Enthroned with Christ in heavenly places, as scripture says, we will look down on our circumstances rather than around. The walls of our earthly existence will not limit our vision. You and I, your church and mine, your people and mine are called to participate and to play a unique part in the great divine plan. We are not biding our time, waiting to go home to heaven. Earth is home and we must bring heaven into our world.

We are one nation, made up of every tribe and tongue. Our salvation is not only individual but corporate and linked to every believer, whether born of God in the past, right here and now, or yet to be born in the future. We are one universal, holy, catholic church spanning all of time and embracing every stream of truth. Many Christians, particularly in new and independent churches, can only see their locality, their group or family, or even only themselves. They are detached, unconcerned and distant from their brothers and sisters elsewhere. This leads to pride if things go well and depression if we fail. We were created to share one another's abundance and participate in one another's need.

Personal salvation, personal holiness, personal resources, my ministry and my church are valid but pitifully small-minded. Jesus is not coming back for a toe or finger, but for a body, a mature and holy bride. Israel understood the truth of corporate salvation, often neglecting their personal walk with God and bringing judgement on themselves. Western Christians, at the other extreme, are individualistic. This, too, is sin.

In the church which my wife and I planted in East London in 1967, God released a wave of creativity. The prophetic Spirit inspired new expressions of worship, music, drama and dance. It was exhilarating, it was fun and it was dangerous. We mostly lived in the same few streets, sharing all that we had. Prophets prophesied and actors acted out what they heard. The singers put the message to words and music which travelled far and wide, where the spoken ministry would never have been welcome.

A few saints meeting in a lounge transferred to the local pub as they grew and became a source of inspiration for a new hymnology. Without realizing we became history-makers by responding to God. "Abba Father," "We Are Being Built Into a Temple," "Jesus Take Me As I Am," "Let Us Open Up Ourselves to One Another," "Let There Be Love Shared Among Us," "Behold How Good and Pleasant It Is," "Praise Him On The Trumpet" are just a few of the songs which poured out. Other New Churches joined in the movement which gave rise to household names in the UK and beyond: Dave Bilbrough, Noel Richards, Graham Kendrick, Sue Rinaldi, Martin Smith . . .

"Bind us Together"

The most widely sung song written in our small house church was "Bind us Together." Translated into many languages, it was sung by thousands of Roman Catholics gathered in St Peter's

Square. One friend travelling in the Himalayas heard the familiar strain coming from a straw hut in a very strange tongue. The songs are the irrefutable evidence of what God did through a bunch of nobodies from Romford, England, who became history-makers.

These hymns, together with hundreds of others written at the time, reflected God's heart for unity – "An Army of Ordinary People," "A Bride All Pure and Holy," "One Body, One Spirit." The prophets and minstrels gave a generation of Christians hope and strength to break out of institutionalism and mediocrity. Looking back over the churches' past, individual pioneers, small companies of misunderstood saints and persecuted minorities, like little Davids, have faced the mighty Goliaths of formalism, unbelief and hypocrisy and won. We are called to be part of this historic, mould-breaking company until Jesus comes.

A cloud of witnesses

Since the dark ages the Lord has been calling his people back to their roots in simpler, uncomplicated spirituality. The red line of grace tracing the Spirit's pursuit of the Father's purposes is in each generation. The shaking, breaking and refining of the church takes place so that the beauty of Jesus' character and the power of his majesty are finally displayed.

Seven times the refiner's fire is applied to the crucible. Seven times the dross is skimmed away until the craftsman sees his image reflected in the molten metal. The Reformation and the even more radical Anabaptist movement, the Great Evangelical Awakening, the Pentecostal revival, Charismatic renewal and the recent New or House Church movement springing up around the world, are all results of the purifying process so Christ is preached and Jesus glorified in every place.

Hebrews 11 reminds us of our history-making heritage. We see the giants of our faith: some achieved great things for the kingdom, others died persecuted and alone. Their mighty deeds and their ability to sacrifice could act as a deterrent, for such bravery is beyond the reach of ordinary saints. However, the next chapter urges us to look to the source of their inspiration. Being surrounded by this cloud of witnesses, we are encouraged to fix our eyes, not on them, but on Jesus! If we see only the heroines and heroes of our past, we will be overwhelmed, but if we see the Lord, their hidden reservoir of strength, we will be empowered.

The majority of those outstanding women and men of God were raised up to bring the people back to God. It was always his desire that the whole nation should be "the light to the Gentiles," not one or two exceptional individuals. At the time of Jesus the witnesses were of a different order altogether: a widow with her mite; a harlot with her perfume; a Roman centurion; a woman with an issue of blood; a cleansed leper returning thanks; a dying thief; a tax collector. Here ordinary people are finding their place in God's roll of honour.

The day of the streams is over ...

So it is with the church. God has raised up key people to put us back on course, but his intention has ever been that together we should be the "city set on a hill," a "light to the world." The day of the superstar is over, the day of the galaxy is here. The day of the streams is over, the day of the river is here. The day of the many bodies, denominations, works and societies is over, the day of the one body is here. Francis Frangipane, author and speaker from the USA, warns us that "Jesus is coming back for a bride not a harem!"

Together we can do it! Joined by the Spirit with those from

every nation, we can be history-makers. We can make a difference, turn cities upside down, challenge unrighteous governments, heal the sick, feed the hungry and set captives free. God's people are ready, willing to lift up the cross of Jesus whatever the cost in shaking to ourselves, our churches or our streams.

We begin to see the fulfillment of this vision in many parts of the world as revival is rewriting the history books of nations and continents. The old "mission" frontiers have become the primary centres of Christian advancement. "Receiving nations" are becoming "sending nations" as a new missionary force is being released.

In the UK we see the signs as hundreds of thousands attend "Alpha" groups all over Britain. In recent years thousands of men and women in our prisons have come to Christ. Black leaders are now producing the fastest-growing churches and thousands of black Christians gather for nights of prayer. New forms of Sunday school with hundreds of children attending are taking off, even though the statistics say "Sunday schools are over." More and more churches are coming together in prayer and reconciliation to serve their communities without regard for personal gain. Now is the time to:

> Rise up church with broken wings,
> Fill this place with songs again,
> Of our God who reigns on high:
> By his grace again we'll fly.

> Martin Smith © 1995 Curious ? Music UK,
> by kind permission of Furious? Records

CHAPTER 5

A DIFFERENT KIND OF PERSON

I don't spit an' I don't chew,
I don't do the things you do –
'Cos I'm a holy person.
I don't laugh an' I don't cry,
My pie's in the sky when I die –
'Cos I'm a holy person.
I don't dance, I don't jump
And I never get the hump –
'Cos I'm a holy person.
I don't smoke, I don't drink,
I don't even ever think –
'Cos I'm a holy person.

No chocolate cake and no TV,
No extra-marital activity,
No sex, no drugs, no beer in mugs,
No Chinese food, no Bombay duck,
No lottery, no stroke of luck,
No motor-bike, no fast Porsche car,
No sweets, no cake an' no Mars Bar,
No pent-house flat or Abbey House
No fur coats or silken blouse,
No strawberry jam, no white-sliced bread,
No nothin now – 'cos now I'm dead!   J.N.

A different kind of holiness

Although one might think that holiness has always been a high agenda item in every church, we must conclude that present levels of holy living among Christians have failed to impress the world in recent years. This will not be the case in the future.

Moynagh in *Changing World, Changing Church*, says:

> It is not hard to imagine church in the West sprawled like a beached whale, eventually dying because it has been cut off from society. All that needs to happen is for congregations to persist with what they do now.

Jesus was not known for his conservative clothing, religious ways or eccentric, legalistic lifestyle. He looked and behaved like most other ordinary people. What singled him out was the Dove, God's Holy Spirit. John the Baptist said he would not have known Jesus if it were not for the Spirit descending upon him (John 1:33). So what can we recognize in Jesus' walk in the Spirit that we should nurture in our lives, so we too can be the kind of people that will make a difference?

Losing alternatives

"Heads I win, tails you lose," are just the kind of odds the devil is pleased to offer. He gives us a choice but the outcome is always favourable to him. Holiness is no exception. He'll let you win the battle against the flesh providing you pray the proud prayer, "I thank you Lord that I'm not as other men!" He'll let you believe in the grace of God as long as it's the sentimental kind that overlooks sin and makes no demand for a change of values or lifestyle.

Legalism and licence are two ends of a stick; they separate us from God and close the door in our lives to the saving power of the gospel. The deception is complete when we believe we are holy because of what we do *not* do, or we are forgiven in spite of the fact that we practise habitual sin. No wonder the world is unimpressed with our God when we convey his message as, "thou shalt not!" or "never mind, then."

The third way

With Jesus there is another option apart from self-effort or acquiescence. He said, "I am the way!" His message, "Go on, you can do it, I'm with you!" enables us to be a totally different kind of people – Jesus people, holy people. It is truly "good news." Augustus Toplady's fine hymn puts it well when it speaks of the "double cure":

> Rock of Ages, cleft for me,
> Let me hide myself in thee!
> Let the water and the blood,
> From thy riven side which flowed,
> Be of sin the double cure –
> Cleanse me from its guilt and power.

We are not only forgiven, wonderful though that is; we are empowered! This kind of people cannot be ignored; their lives demand a response. They are different and, like Jesus, they will be either loved or hated. They are not different because they live in some rarefied heavenly atmosphere. The very opposite, they disturbingly bring God, Jesus and heaven right into the ordinary, humdrum things of everyday life. Neil T. Anderson in his book *The Common Made Holy*, written with Robert Saucy and published by Monarch, puts it this way – "It is not *what* we do that determines who we are, it is *who* we are that determines what we do."

God's nature is holy: that's why he behaves in holiness. Isaiah 6:3 declares, "holy, holy, holy is the Lord God Almighty," three holies indicating that each person of the Trinity is holy and will work with us to make us holy as he is holy, until "the whole earth is full of his glory."

Sadly, much of our religion is cosmetic, tarting up the outside or making us feel good on the inside. Neither action deals with the human condition of fallenness and sin. Dallas Willard, in *The Divine Conspiracy* published by Fount, asks, "Can we seriously believe that God would establish a plan for us that essentially bypasses the awesome needs of present human life and leaves human character untouched?" He powerfully underlines the New Testament teaching that "this kingdom is not something to be 'accepted' now and enjoyed later, but something to be entered now."

Lost and without hope

Negative holiness looks good from a distance, just as sentimental grace feels good for a moment, but neither will satisfy a heart crying out for reality. The truth may be painful to receive but it will set us free. The late Jamie Buckingham summed it up in the title of one of his books – *The Truth will set you free . . . but first it will make you miserable*. That we have misery first is an indicator that we are not convinced that the old life is death. We have not experienced the ultimate disillusionment with ourselves, that without God we could not be worse off or more condemned. We are totally lost without Jesus – there is no hope outside of the cross.

Paul understood this. He said with conviction, "I am the foremost of sinners" (1 Timothy 1:15, RSV). Accepting this truth releases us to rely completely on Jesus and to depend fully on the Holy Spirit and real grace, which not only washes away our filth, but enables us to live the kingdom way. What is the kingdom way? What have we missed that is right under our noses? What were the foundations in Jesus' life that enabled him to avoid temptation and fulfil his destiny to change history?

Immanence

Russian astronauts informed us, "Space is empty – God does not exist out there." Religion, at best, tells us God is remote, and disapproving. Jesus, on the other hand, showed us that God is everywhere, completely involved, interested in every detail of our lives. He enjoyed intimacy with his Father, a friendship which bred trust and security. We need that too, but the God who is everywhere had to manifest himself somewhere in order to be known in that way. Jesus is the bridge. Through his physical body and the indwelling of the Holy Spirit, heaven and earth interact as one. His death removed the barrier – sin is finally and forever gone – we are friends of God!

Now, those of us who accept the atonement, or better *at-one-ment,* become part of the bridge and the kingdom of heaven pours into the world through us! Like Jesus we can announce with boldness, "The kingdom of heaven is at hand," and it is seen and felt among us. Jesus, and therefore God, is the "friend of sinners," we are one with him and he dwells in and with us.

In Jesus, the physical and spiritual realms came together, but faith enables us to "see" the reality. For those who have "seen" God in creation, faith, or anti-faith, is required to believe that there is no God. Russian space explorers made a superficial recce of heaven before declaring what was in the best interests of their government, but for those who have "seen", the heavens are the evidence of God's existence and they speak endlessly of his creative power.

You could say John Noble does not exist: we have dissected his body; he is not there. But those who have touched my soul know differently. For good or bad, their memory of me cannot be obliterated. We may not physically be able to "see" the soul or spirit realm, but the evidence of its existence is all around in the fruits of love or hatred depending on our source. The kingdom of heaven is at hand! God is nearer than breath; he is at the door of our hearts, waiting to be invited in and be known by us.

Transcendence

In spite of this wonderful intimacy, we are not to be over-familiar with God. He is our friend, our Abba, Daddy, a Father with whom we can laugh and cry and be at home, but he is also creator of the universe, the all-powerful, all-knowing One present everywhere. This paradox, this contradiction, makes our God amazing, fantastic and such a thrilling person to know. The dawning of this truth finally broke Job and brought deliverance from his all-consuming preoccupation with his predicament.

The story of Job in the Old Testament tells of the struggles this upright man encountered with the seeming inconsistencies of the just God he worshipped and the incredibly unjust suffering he experienced. It shows the battle going on in heaven for his soul, of which he was totally unaware. It describes his frustration with "friends" who tried to help him in his desperate search for answers.

Finally, when all the talk was over, God spoke out of the shaking of a violent storm. He came to sit where Job sat on the ash heap, just as he came to Elijah in the cave. My guess is that once again the Lord spoke with a still small voice but with cutting truth as a genuine friend does, lancing the boil of resentment burning in Job's soul. "Where were you when I laid the earth's foundations?" (Job 38:4). If there was a word for "whoops!" in Hebrew, Job would have said it, but he wisely remained silent while God give him a personal lesson on creation and how it works.

All Job's arguments melted in the presence of this awesome creator-God, who loved him too much to leave him to die in a slough of self-pity and despair. The love and discipline dealt with his sin and Job was free: "Surely I spoke of things I did not understand, things too wonderful for me to know . . . My ears had heard of you but now my eyes have seen you. Therefore I despise myself and repent . . ." (Job 42:3–6). In our intimate relationship with Jesus, we must never lose sight of his exalted place above all as King of Kings and Lord of Lords.

Empowered to live

Romans 2:4 tells us: "God's kindness (or 'goodness' AV) leads us toward repentance." The incredible truth is that the God of the universe has a deep and personal interest in me. He loves me so much he gave his most treasured possession, his Son, for me. This reality deposits in me the power to change. I hear his voice urging me onward, "Go on my son, my daughter, you can do it. I am with you and in you to work the will of my Father."

Colossians 3:1 & 5 picks up this spirit of encouragement as Paul cries: "Since, then, you have been raised with Christ, set your hearts on things above . . . Put to death . . . ['put off' AV] whatever belongs to your earthly nature: sexual immorality, impurity, lust, evil desires and greed." Then in verse 12 he calls us to "clothe yourselves with ["put on" AV] compassion, kindness, humility, gentleness and patience . . ."

Jesus is not asking us to do anything he has not already done. In Luke 4:1–12 we see Jesus, filled with the Holy Spirit, overcoming temptation in his own life before moving in the power of the Spirit to overcome on our behalf. Hebrews 4:15 assures us we have an example in Jesus as "one who has been tempted in every way, just as we are – yet was without sin."

The presence of Jesus and the indwelling of the Spirit give us power to enter a process of "being transformed into his likeness with ever-increasing glory" (2 Corinthians 3:18). As we give way to his chastening, we are changed, imperceptibly at times, into a reflection of Jesus: a ray of hope in a world of darkness and despair.

Ten thousand times ten thousand

Thank God for every life transformed; every tiny candle lit. As evil draws its veil of darkness round the world, the pinpoints of light which have always been there begin to flicker like twinkling stars in the evening twilight sky. Thousands upon thousands waiting, like players in the wings, to take their place on the firmament's vast stage to share their story of grace. Then, together with creation, in a final extravaganza of praise, they fill the sky singing with one voice, "The heavens declare the glory of God; the skies proclaim the work of his hands" (Psalm 19:1).

In holiness we were made to be together, each in our appointed place, set apart for the Lord. Lovingly and uniquely fashioned by him to blend the colours, shapes, sounds and aromas of our lives in glorious and beautiful array. So there is movement and flexibility in glory but also permanence. Our God assures us, "Never will I leave you; never will I forsake you" (Hebrews 13:5), and Jesus does the same, so we learn to live in commitment to one another, too.

The everlasting kingdom which cannot be shaken will produce eternal qualities in us. Wherever we are, wherever we go, we will dwell in an expanding circle of love from which betrayal, disloyalty and divorce are banished. The power of our message will grow in direct proportion to the reality and visibility of the kingdom community.

Three stages of relationships

As we are joined together by the Spirit and find our place in the body of Christ our relationships evolve through three stages. First a superficial level or *honeymoon* as we experience the thrill of discovering our common identity together as family and friends. All is light and happiness until we see one another's "feet of clay."

At this point we enter the *disillusionment* stage. Did God really join me to this person or group? To know the blessing of mature and lasting friendship we must press on through disillusionment by sharing lovingly and honestly while holding on to one another, warts and all. Then we enter *reality*, where we know all there is to know about one another and yet fully accept each other in love and respect. Neither our differences nor our strengths separate us or keep us from affirming one another and working hand in hand for Jesus and the good of his people.

Christine and I have always lived with an extended family by choice. One of the happiest times in our lives was during the early days of the tiny fellowship which centred upon our home. Along with our five kids we had 12 others living with us in our five-bedroomed house with only one bathroom! Bunks and put-away beds were squeezed into every corner, and we shared everything together.

A recipe for disaster? Not at all! Naturally we had difficulties, but because we lived in openness, love and truth, willing to accept discipline, it was a time of blessing and growth. We were reversing the trend of fragmentation in our society. Soon we were 200 living within a couple of blocks and making our mark in the community, then five or six related groups sprang up within a few miles.

Rattled as well as shaken

In 1984, after 17 wonderful years, the Lord allowed the enemy to sift us in order that we might go deeper with him. Our focus subtly moved from Jesus to our relationships, which we began to take for granted. Our invitation also moved from, "Come and be joined to Jesus," to "Come and be joined to us." The gospel of Christ had become the gospel of the church. That period of shaking was the most severe I have experienced, and we were devastated. We will always walk with a limp and carry the pain of many precious friendships seemingly lost forever.

The testing led us to return to the centrality of Jesus, the cross and his gospel of grace and forgiveness. Sadly, one of the side effects of reacting to over-emphasis on relationships seems to be a loss of the throbbing community life. Middle-class attitudes take over with their values of careers, home ownership, education (none bad in themselves) which dull creativity, flexibility and innovation.

The African American spiritual "Dem bones, dem bones, dem dry bones" is never far from mind when I think about relationships. The story of connecting bones in Ezekiel 37 has been a source of revelation and encouragement. First, we were inspired by the knowledge that dead bones could live and be brought together in a body, clothed with flesh and filled with breath.

We foolishly thought this had been accomplished when we experienced renewal and discovered like-minded friends. What a thrill it was, but we completely overlooked the shake-out that would be necessary before we could find our proper place. This takes time and commitment – "there's no gain without pain" as the saying goes, and remains a hard lesson to learn. Perhaps the fullness of this will only be received when Breath or Spirit comes upon us corporately. Then the army of God will arise!

Still running

Thankfully the church we planted survived and is growing again. I remember the Lord graciously making me face up to the words I had so often ministered in my naivety and enthusiasm. "If all we have built should fall apart what would we do?" I said, "We would pick up the pieces and start again because the revelation of 'dwelling together in unity' is from God!" Those words came back to me and strangely provided a rock in those troubled days, on which we could build again.

We still have a long way to go but, as the late Ern Baxter said when confronted with that thought – "Yes, we have a long way to go – but thank God we left!" Jesus went ahead and sent the Holy Spirit so we can be the different kind of people he can use to build a different kind of church to make the world a different kind of place.

PART II

The leadership of change

CHAPTER 6

OUT OF PRISON – THE NEW APOSTOLIC CHURCH!

Spiritual leadership lost – the church in prison

In spite of the explosion of life, dynamic evangelism, prayer and miracles which broke out in the early church, in three to four hundred years Satan had laid the foundations of a prison which would keep the good news under wraps for centuries. Brick by brick the walls were put in place which would hold God's people captive in the dark cells of the establishment.

The sin of the Nicolaitans (meaning conquer or rule over, Revelation 2:6 & 15) prevailed. They were a group of corrupt leaders who drew people to themselves. The resulting, unbiblical, division between priest and congregation meant the masses were cut off from a direct relationship with Jesus. This situation was worsened because the Bible was not readily available to combat the teachings which locked people into such unscriptural authority.

Centuries later people were controlled by ignorance, superstition and guilt and the imposition of penances and indulgences was rife. Nevertheless, the truth could not be totally contained. Some rebel prisoners refused to be silent, while others managed to escape their chains to undermine the devilish strategy. The blood of these martyrs cried out for justice and their prayers were heard in heaven.

The process which reduced the church from pulsating life to coma was carefully devised. The foundational ministries of apostle and prophet were either martyred or marginalized. The balance of authority shifted from a local, relationally based oversight team with outside spiritual input, to a centralized organization. The mobile apostolic teams, led by pioneering fathers who planted the churches and ordained local leadership, were replaced by a static maintenance-dominated administration. Evangelists did not flourish and soon the pastoral and teaching gifts foundered. Power fell into the hands of treasurers and administrators.

The battle for supremacy led to the emergence of an immoral, politically motivated leadership which became centred upon one person. The earthly marriage of convenience between church and state usurped the planned heavenly wedding between Jesus and his bride. Christianity became fashionable, a means of advancement, and paganism was absorbed or outlawed. At the time of Augustine coercion by the state was used to bring "heretics" in line. "Compel them to come in" (Luke 14:23, AV) was used to justify such actions, thereby giving supposed scriptural authority to a whole host of evils, including the crusades and the inquisition.

By medieval times the idea of a church which was not part of the state was unthinkable. This is why groups such as the Lollards were regarded as a threat to both church and state. Finally scripture was confined to a dead language only a privileged few could understand. The incarceration was complete. The church of Jesus Christ was well and truly jailed. Jim Thwaites in *The Church Beyond the Congregation* comments,

"The dark ages descended to blanket the Christian church in Platonic mist and empire-building arrogance."

Dark ages

With God's Kingdom-people disempowered it was open day on the world stage. The rise of Islam and the establishment of the church as a secular power meant the control of Jerusalem became a key issue. For Jews, Arabs and nominal Christians this city would be a jewel in the crown of world domination. With their belief that mankind is destined to rule the earth, the three monotheistic religions each assumed they were God's chosen people for the task: the Jews through their coming Messiah, the Arabs and Christians by force.

Through bloody conflict, much pain and suffering, Islam established itself in the place where Israel once flourished and where Christianity was born. In their blindness these contenders for Jerusalem missed the fact that the Holy City, through a coalition with Rome against the Son of God, had become "the great city, which is figuratively called Sodom and Egypt, where also their Lord was crucified" (Revelation 11:8). Through acts of harlotry with worldly powers, Jerusalem was identified as Babylon itself. This is a salutary reminder that God is not committed to thrones, temples, or cities but to the humble, contrite hearts that seek his face.

Thank God, this is not the end of the story. The Holy Spirit kept alive the dream of a new heaven and new earth with a New Jerusalem at the centre. Men and women moved by the Spirit began to pray for the reversal of the process which led to their captivity. So, while the early church moved from clarity to confusion over centuries, we now see her, over a similar timescale, travelling from confusion to the clarity Jesus intended. Small rumblings became mighty shakings and the walls which had held the church for so long began to fall. "The Shaking" was under way!

Unmasking the Bible

The great Bible translation movement started in the 16th century and continues today with 2,000 tongues to go! The accessibility of scripture led to the restoration of the pulpit and the teaching ministry. Luther's realization that justification was by faith in the grace of God opened the door for the great evangelical missionary movements of the 18th and 19th centuries.

The prison crumbled, the debris fell away and a new kind of building was revealed – a living temple made without hands. The colouring on the map of world religions changed as the gospel went out to the ends of the earth.

The recovery of the teacher and evangelist was followed by a worldwide outpouring of the Holy Spirit at the beginning of the 20th century and the Pentecostal movement was born. This flowed into Charismatic renewal affecting every stream and denomination. Now the supernatural gifts of the Spirit are within reach of every believer and Christ's gift of the prophet is back in church. The growing "unity of the Spirit" (Ephesians 4:3) must soon give way to "unity in the faith" (v.13), both necessary for God's people to "become mature, attaining to the whole measure of the fulness of Christ." At last we've arrived? No, the shaking must continue yet. A unifying ministry is needed to bring all the extremes in the body together.

Apostolic leadership

The most incredible thing about Jesus is his ability to reconcile the irreconcilable. In him all the contrasts of life and truth are held in tension. Mercy and judgement kiss; grace and truth blend in perfect harmony; male and female are united; black, white, Jew and Greek stand as one. In him, teachers and prophets find equal expression with pastors and evangelists. Those so often at odds with one another find peace.

Hebrews 3:1 describes Jesus as "the apostle" whose calling we share. He is unique, but we participate in his ministry and anointing. The most important quality of Jesus and therefore of apostolic ministry is not church planting, foundation laying or working miracles, but reconciliation. Apostles bring order out of chaos. God began with creation; Jesus continued on the cross, and we pursue this same calling to unite all things in Christ!

Jesus was first and foremost "the apostle." Before he was prophet, evangelist, pastor or teacher, he was "the one sent forth on a mission of reconciliation from the Father." Of all the ministry gifts expressed in him, this was of primary importance and was necessary to begin foundational and building work. It's clear that when Jesus passed on his five-fold ministry to the church as gifts of his ascension (Ephesians 4:11), he gave first, in order of seniority not superiority, the gift of apostle – "first of all apostles" (1 Corinthians 12:28). Why should he do this?

The answer is simple. Apostles or master-builders bring together the diverse skills required for construction to begin (1 Corinthians 3:10). They have an overview of the house, which is necessary if the different gifts are to work in harmony. They carry a concern that the work is completed accurately in all its detail – "exactly like the pattern I will show you" (Exodus 25:9). Not a draughtsman's plan, nor a Frankenstein creation but a perfect, living body. For this reason an apostle must be a facilitator, and a visionary. Tony Morton, who leads an apostolic team in the South of England, is clear on the primacy and visionary nature of apostles – "all apostles must be prophetic, but not all prophets are apostolic."

Like Jesus, apostles will give their lives so the church becomes a suitable dwelling for God and a vehicle through which the image of God's Son is expressed. In churches where foundations are laid by a teacher or pastor or by an evangelist they will be lop-sided, emphasizing the particular concern of the ministry. Now it is the time for strong, full-orbed churches built on apostolic and prophetic foundations.

Passing on the anointing and the commission

It would be foolish to suggest there were no apostles at other times in church history, but today the renewal is moving us to a fresh dimension of restoration. A new apostolic era is coming which will ensure the anointing on Jesus, which he imparted to his disciples, is transferred to the whole body of Christ. The apostolic ministry, first to disappear, will be last to reappear and will lead the church into her most productive period of mission as the corporate apostle, sent to every corner of the globe.

Psalm 133 is a profound prophetic statement of the dynamic effects of a community joined in life and purpose:

How good and pleasant it is when brothers live together in unity!
It is like precious oil poured on the head, running down on the
    beard,
running down on Aaron's beard, down upon the collar of his robes.
It is as if the dew of Hermon were falling on Mount Zion.
For there the Lord bestows his blessing, even life for evermore.

Such unity is a magnet to God's blessing. The anointing oil, a unique and fragrant blend of spices, was specially prepared. This was a holy compound set apart for a purpose: the one who used it for anything else would be cut off (Exodus 30:22–33). It was generously poured over Aaron's head, and ran down his beard, saturated the garments which covered his whole body and dripped on to the floor. The aroma filled the place where the priest carried out his duties. The imagery points us to Christ and his church.

This oil, symbol of the Holy Spirit, is poured on Christ the Head. From him it runs down to the shoulders, the burden bearers, his chosen apostles and then on to the whole body. Even the feet are saturated and the perfume lingers wherever we humbly serve Jesus. It is in this place of unity that the Lord commands the blessing of life for evermore.

The apostolic power and anointing of the gospel flows from Jesus to his delegated leaders and is released through a vibrant, healthy, active body. Jesus' prayer is finally answered, 'I have given them the glory that you gave me, that they may be one as we are one: I in them and you in me. May they be brought to complete unity to let the world know that you sent me . . .' (John 17:22–23).

It has been said that the purpose of leadership in the church is to do itself out of a job. This is true, but not in the sense that leaders will have nothing to do. Rather, delegation will free them to move to other fields of service. This side of heaven there will always be plenty to do to nurture the church and establish it in every stratum of society.

Jesus did not come as superman, standing alone in majesty and power, but rather bringing many sons to glory. Likewise apostles and prophets were not given to do the work and receive the honour, but "to prepare God's people for works of service" (Ephesians 4:12), to pass on "glory" and dispense power so together we become world changers.

Thwaites in *The Church Beyond the Congregation* insists:

Ministers must equip the saints for every level of their engagement with creation. From the moment of salvation, through the nurture stage, into the time of maturation, restoration and occupation of all created things, the ministry gifts must stand with the saints.

God's people are his holy nation and royal priesthood. If the good news is to run through the earth in a generation every saint must be mobilized with the authority of Jesus. The head must control the body so the church becomes "the apostle," and also "the prophet," "the evangelist," "the pastor" and "teacher" too. Less than this and we will never fulfil our mission to disciple all nations.

The church is Christ's body

The church really is Christ on earth. He has no other hands to heal with, no other mouth to teach with, no other feet to go with but ours. The church is his secret weapon, the container of his manifold wisdom (Ephesians 3:10). He has no plan B, nothing in reserve if we fail – we're it! He's committed to us and trusts the power at work within us. The apostle Paul knew this – "in all these things we are more than conquerors through him who loved us" (Romans 8:37).

Christ's love, shed abroad in our hearts, transforms and motivates us. It creates the hunger within which drives us to seek his face so we reflect his likeness as he shares his nature with us. All that he is we become. His character and power, his life and ministry, his death and resurrection are all ours. As the Father sent him so he now sends his body, victorious in suffering and success, a new kind of apostle altogether – the ultimate and last before Jesus comes again.

CHAPTER 7

THE FIFTH TRADITION

The continuance of apostles

Apostolic succession is a reality. It is a gift of Jesus to the church through the impartation of the Holy Spirit which often takes place with the laying on of hands. However, the gift is not automatically passed on by those ordained within traditional churches. For example, it is difficult for evangelical, charismatic Christians to believe that an unconverted bishop could impart the Holy Spirit and commission apostles simply because his church has given him the authority. This is dualism and separates the office from the character of the officer.

No, the line of succession is maintained by the Holy Spirit himself. He works with those called by Christ, indwelt by him and who function in mutual submission with all those under the authority of Jesus, the true and only head of the church. So institutional apostles and self-styled apostles must give way to Christ-appointed apostles. Of course there have been many godly leaders in the institutional church over centuries. We praise God for them and all they have done to keep the church on track.

In Scripture we see each member of the Godhead involved in

giving apostles to the church and giving the church as the "apostle" to the world. Jesus was unique, the Chief Apostle sent by the Father (Hebrews 3:1). The 12, "apostles of the Lamb" (Revelation 21:14), were appointed by Jesus, to be with him from the beginning as witnesses to all he did and said. They too are unique as 12, their symbolic number, connects them to the old patriarchal dynasty of Jacob's 12 sons and announces the Kingdom is at hand.

In the Acts we see break-out. Jesus the Apostle sent by the Father empowers and sends the 12; these apostles of Jesus the Lamb, in their turn, lay hands on the many apostles of the Holy Spirit and a startling multiplication takes place. So Father, Son and Holy Spirit are involved together in sending apostles.

Watchman Nee, in *The Normal Christian Church*, points to references in the New Testament which indicate the existence of numerous apostles apart from Paul and the 12. Seven others are actually named, one of whom, Junia, is a woman. Beyond this, 1 Thessalonians 2:6 and 1 Corinthians 15:5–7 obviously refer to others, certainly more than two or three on each occasion. This is remarkable, bearing in mind that the evangelist, a ministry so strongly promoted in the church today, has only one example, Philip. So, while the Holy Spirit remains with us, and there is work to be done to bring the church into the fullness of her ministry, he will raise up apostles to work to this end.

The traditions

In his book *The Household of God* published in London by SCM (1953) and in New York by Friendship (1954), the late Bishop Lesslie Newbigin gave an analysis of traditions which have evolved in the church. He identifies three major streams – Catholic/Sacramental, Protestant/Reformed and Pentecostal/ Charismatic. These reflect the Godhead, the Sacramental revealing the Father heart of God, the Reformed, the Son's concern for truth and the Charismatic, the Spirit's desire to empower. His longing was to see these streams moving alongside one another as one church together.

Inspired by this analysis I come from a different perspective, that of the five-fold ministry of teacher, pastor, evangelist, prophet and apostle of Ephesians 4:11. As Jesus' gift to the church these ministries must function freely to bring the church to her full potential in Christ. The process of the restoration of these gifts during the last 400 years, has reversed the process of decline and has set the church on the glorious road to recovery. Today, we are in the final stages of that recovery and therefore very close to pressing home the victory of the cross in our generation.

1. Sacramental/pastoral

This tradition, expressed primarily through the Catholic and orthodox churches, established the Eucharist as its focus, its strengths in devotion, worship and holiness. The altar is a central feature and the *pastor* or priest plays the key role. The worst aspects of this tradition are ecclesiolatry, or worship of the church, and abuse of the sacrament as the church comes between the people and a direct relationship to Jesus. This produces passivity and dependence on an up-front, one-man (emphasis on one-*man*) ministry.

2. Reformed/teaching

The Reformed tradition, outcome of the first major shaking the church had experienced for centuries, focused attention on the Bible. Its strengths were preaching, exposition and a quest for truth. The pulpit was the central feature and the *teacher* played the key role. The weaknesses occurred because there was overemphasis on intellect, and the result was bibliolatry, or Bible worship. The Trinity became Father, Son and Holy Scripture, which led to pride, legalism and empty worship, with the church and her practices mostly irrelevant to the people she sought to reach.

3. Missionary/evangelistic

The Missionary tradition was a natural progression of the Reformation, since truth understood must be proclaimed. The open Bible revealed our reason for being. The "Great Awakening" focused on fulfilling the Great Commission. Its strengths were evangelistic zeal and a willingness to sacrifice all to preach the gospel to every people. The field was the central feature, the *evangelist* was the key player and under this ministry the church grew by leaps and bounds.

The weaknesses were seen later. The gospel message, unwittingly mixed in its application with culture, was imposed through paternalism and Western imperialism. The evangelistic ministries of the day were marginalized by the church, giving rise to missionary societies and a welter of new denominations.

4. Charismatic/prophetic

The Charismatic tradition was in evidence throughout the church's history but began in earnest with the Pentecostal outpourings at the beginning of the 20th century. It advanced through renewal movements from the sixties to the present. The main focus was the Holy Spirit and his supernatural manifestations. The restoration of prophecy and healing, with other gifts of the Spirit, were the strengths. This fresh encouragement to the church came when humanism, the enlightenment and rationalism had done serious damage to religious belief. The tide of doubt turned and today there is more openness to the gospel than at any time in history.

A central feature of this tradition was the "tarrying" meeting where the Holy Spirit was given room to move. The *prophet* has played a key role, although all-member "body ministry" is encouraged. The weaknesses are over-emphasis on experience and neglect of Bible teaching. In addition, personality cults have frequently laid an unhealthy focus on spiritual phenomena and financial or material prosperity.

Nevertheless, the effects of Pentecostal/Charismatic renewal have seriously reshaped the church and its geography. Nations which had virtually no Christian presence, such as Korea, have grown to 30% Christian and in some South American countries to an even greater percentage.

5. Radical/apostolic

The pattern of gradual loss followed by gradual recovery continues. In this development we must acknowledge groups such as Montanists and Anabaptists, who kept the "Radical Tradition" alive. We would do well to learn from them.

The birth pangs of this modern apostolic movement began with the Pentecostal revival, which produced a keen interest in the ministry and the nature of the church. This was nurtured by writers like G.H. Lang, Austin Sparks, Roland Allen and Watchman Nee, and further pioneered by the house church movements in China and the United Kingdom. The weaknesses of this tradition will be a wrong perception of authority, authority abuse and kingdom building. However, as Paul explained, the false will serve to strengthen and verify the true (1 Corinthians 11:19).

The time is right for a full-blooded "Radical Apostolic" tradition that will take the best elements of the previous four traditions and bind them together in a final, strong witness to Christ's character and power in the earth. The focus will be the King and the kingdom, laying solid foundations based on right relationships with God and one another.

The unique feature of the Radical tradition will be the flexible, mobile apostolic teams drawn from diverse ministries which readily adapt to meet the different needs of churches and prepare them for ministry. The primary role is that of *apostles* who, together with all the other ministries, will facilitate unity with diversity, bridging the gap between different personalities, cultures and church traditions.

Accelerating interest

Having moved from ostracism, to criticism, to reluctant acceptance, there is now a growing excitement about the apostolic ministry in the church. In the UK it has been a battle to ignite a positive enquiry into this neglected ministry during the last 35 years. As recently as 1999 Peter Lyne's book *First Apostles, Last Apostles* was turned down by a leading publisher on the basis that there is no interest in the subject. Fortunately Sovereign World saw its importance and it is now available in Britain and elsewhere.

On the other hand in the USA, with their ability to package and market anything, I understand you can obtain an "Apostolic Starter Kit" for the reasonable price of $62! Somewhere between these extremes a genuine and determined effort will emerge, inspired by the Spirit, to establish this ministry at the centre of the church's expansion programme worldwide. May God grant us the wisdom and courage to recognize his hand in the earthquakes, winds and fires which are shaking, shaping and preparing us for such a time.

The fifth tradition

TRADITION	FOCUS	MINISTRY	BEST FEATURE	WORST FEATURE
1. SACRAMENTAL	THE SACRAMENTS AND THE PRIEST	PASTOR	DEVOTION TO JESUS AND THE CHURCH	ECCLESIOLATRY – WORSHIP OF THE CHURCH – PASSIVITY
2. REFORMED	THE BIBLE AND THE PULPIT	TEACHER	KNOWLEDGE OF THE SCRIPTURES	BIBLIOLATRY – WORSHIP OF THE BIBLE – THEORETICAL
3. MISSIONARY	THE GREAT COMMISSION AND THE MISSIONARY MOVEMENT	EVANGELIST	REACHING THE UNREACHED	EXPORT AND IMPOSITION OF CULTURE
4. CHARISMATIC	THE BAPTISM AND GIFTS OF THE HOLY SPIRIT	PROPHET	BODY MINISTRY	THE PERSONALITY, MANIFESTATIONS AND PROSPERITY CULTS
5. RADICAL	CHURCH FOUNDATIONS, RELATIONSHIPS AND THE END TIMES	APOSTLE & APOSTOLIC TEAM	LOCAL AND REGIONAL TEAM MINISTRY	AUTHORITY ABUSE AND KINGDOM BUILDING

Note: I acknowledge the "Radical Tradition" has a thin red line of continuity throughout history. Mostly this tradition was unrecognized and at different times carried elements of some or all the other traditions within it.

CHAPTER 8

VANISHING APOSTLES?

Rejection

From earliest times the ministry of apostle has been under
attack. Imprisonment, flogging, persecution and martyrdom
were commonplace. Few in the early church aspired to be apostles because of the pain and rejection involved: they were
seldom given the respect their calling deserved. Perhaps this
lack of popularity was because apostles confronted passivity,
weeded out sin and kept the saints from settling down.
Gradually the ministry lost its influence and was forgotten in
the "success" of the church. Who needs a coach when you're
winning all the trophies and there's no opposition?

As a response to the widespread rediscovery of scripture, and
the questions raised as a result of its availability, theologians
emerged to maintain the status quo. Issues such as slavery,
apartheid, male superiority, the nature of grace, spiritual gifts
and the priesthood of every believer were manipulated to keep
power in the hands of the white ruling classes, not always as a
conscious act but more the result of carnal motivation.

Spiritual leadership which threatened the establishment was

quickly discredited or removed. The roots of these devilish doctrines run deep into our Western cultures and require major spiritual surgery to remove. To this day they are obstacles in the minds of many sincere seekers after truth.

The theory

One such obstacle has been an ingenious teaching known as "the theory of the vanishing apostles." This teaching is responsible for a great deal of confusion. It goes something like this:

After Judas betrayed Jesus and committed suicide, the disciples got together and, realizing their need of a replacement, sought out two men. They did not bother to seek the Lord and used a most unscriptural method to determine which of the two should succeed Judas – they drew lots! The result of this was that Matthias took the place of Judas and was never heard of again. Paul was evidently God's choice to fill the gap: he himself said that he was a man born out of due time 1 Corinthians 15:8 (AV). He did more for the church than any other apostle and was in fact the last apostle, completing their number without further additions. These 12 established the church amongst the Jews, the Samaritans and the Gentiles and represent the sum total of apostles for all time. The New Testament was entirely written or commissioned by the apostles and no other men could possibly match their calling and the miracles they performed. Their writings were infallible!

This is a formidable argument, until we look behind the reasoning to what the Bible really teaches. Let's take it point by point:

The mistake of choosing Matthias

Nowhere in scripture is there any indication that the 11 disciples made a mistake in selecting Joseph and Matthias. The qualification for the replacement of Judas was that he must have been with Jesus from the beginning (Acts 1:21–22). This was not true of Paul: although he did get revelation direct from Jesus (Acts 26:15–16) he could not qualify as an apostle of the Lamb in this way.

Unscriptural lots

Lots were drawn in the Old Testament without rebuke from God. Some scholars suggest that the Urim and Thummim, by which priests determined the Lord's will on certain matters, was a system of lots. As the Holy Spirit had not yet been given, and this was the last time scripture records lots being used, the method was perfectly acceptable to God. After Pentecost, the Holy Spirit's anointing was given to "teach us all things."

It is inconceivable that those godly men and women gathering in the upper room, being of one accord, could have the Holy Spirit bless them in such a wonderful way had they been disobedient. They would have been rebuked by the Lord, and repented of the sin. There would then have been only 11, and Peter would have been recorded as standing up with the ten (Acts 2:14).

Matthias's ineffective ministry

Matthias is not the only apostle who is not mentioned after Pentecost. Thomas, Bartholomew, Andrew, Matthew and Simon were all present in the upper room, but none of them is referred to again in scripture. Nevertheless, later the 12 are given as the foundation stones of the New Jerusalem (Revelation 21:14). We cannot assume that these men were not used by God. Rather we must believe that the Holy Spirit did not choose to record their particular roles for some reason.

Paul, the real twelfth man . . .

Nowhere does the Bible suggest that Paul was the Lord's replacement for Judas. The phrase "born out of due time" (AV) in the Greek means that his was an abortive or untimely birth and may reveal Paul's frustration that he was not part of the original team – he had been born too late.

. . . and the end of the line

The idea that Paul was the last apostle is unfounded. We have already said that a number of other apostles are mentioned in scripture and still others are implied. In Acts 14:3–4 Barnabas is called an apostle, with Paul; in Galatians 1:19 James, the Lord's brother, is named an apostle; 1 Thessalonians 2:6 refers to Paul, Silas (or Silvanus) and Timothy as apostles. Ephesians 4 points out that all ministries, including apostles, will function until the body of Christ comes to the unity of faith and the fullness of Jesus. We have not quite reached that position yet. J.B. Lightfoot in his commentary on Galatians says that the word apostle "is not so used as to lend any countenance to the idea that it is in any way restricted to the twelve."

Infallible writers

Luke and Mark's gospels, Acts and possibly Hebrews, were not written by any of the apostles. This shows that there were others who were "inspired" to record God's word. There is no reason to believe these men were instructed or supervised by the apostles: they were free agents. The idea that certain men were granted special ability to produce infallible writings is quite wrong. The men were not infallible; indeed some are noted in the Bible as having made mistakes.

When they wrote, it was because they had something they wanted to say, and the Holy Spirit saw to it that what they wrote was inspired and preserved. All the credit is His! Indeed, the great apostle Paul writes, "I *think* that I too have the Spirit of God" (1 Corinthians 7:40), about a certain point of behaviour.

By placing apostles in such elevated positions we have made

it impossible to recognize the calling in ordinary people today. Jesus called simple fisher-folk and made them founders of the church. The Holy Spirit will continue the trend but we limit him through false humility and unbelief. If we expect all apostles to be of the same stature as Paul we will lose the Timothys and the Barnabases.

Authority in the church

The extremes in Catholicism and Protestantism have both failed to produce the right kind of authority in the church, the one by investing absolute authority in one man, the other by allowing every individual equal authority. Talking with Father Tom Forrest, a Catholic priest well known in renewal circles, a fun loving and very approachable man, I questioned him about the infallibility of the Pope. "Yes," he replied, "every hundred years or so we have to come to terms with some papal edict. But it seems to me that every evangelical is his own pope and makes infallible statements every week!"

God intended that, through prayer, relationships, trust and recognition, we should see a plurality of leadership emerge, based on genuine gifts coupled with a willingness to serve. It will function by hearing God together and through mutual submission, not equality. "One-man ministry" will be banished at both local and extra-local levels. The all-powerful or overburdened pastor and the independent, unaccountable, itinerant superstar will become things of the past and leadership will work to empower the people.

Apostolic teams will network within nations and around the world. They will respect and submit to one other and to the local leaders they serve, working together within the limits of their callings and commissioning. Local eldership teams will be supported by these mobile apostles and will become true shepherds to the sheep because of mutual trust and interdependence. Final authority will not rest in the hands of one person or even a team, but in the corporate wisdom of the gathered church, but more of this later.

The unimportance of titles

So, with the mystery of vanishing apostles solved, we expect to see them reappear. Actually, the ministry of apostle has always been around, although in some circles where the present existence of apostles is denied the term is used retrospectively of spiritual giants who have passed on. Of course, we are not looking for titles to paint on vestry doors or parade in magazines, but rather to acknowledge God-given gifts and make room for their wisdom and leadership.

CHAPTER 9

APOSTLES TODAY

Nothing has stirred more interest in Charismatic circles today than the restoration of the five-fold ministries that Paul mentions in Ephesians 4.

Vinson Synon, Chairman of the North American
Renewal Services Committee

"Evangelist" is not the only option

In Britain Charismatic renewal began to affect the church in the late fifties. At that time, if you felt called to ministry the only alternative to becoming a pastor was to be an evangelist, and evangelists were treated with suspicion. Actually, there was also an élite class of revered gentlemen, mainly from the Plymouth Brethren, who had somehow achieved the lofty status of "itinerant Bible teacher." No one knows how this happened or how they survived financially: they "lived by faith" and never talked about money. George Müller, of Bristol, was the prototype.

The evangelist was thought to be of low character and rebellious, usually wearing outlandish clothes and working among the youth. He (it was never a woman) might lure away young people with coffee and questionable music and start his own church in opposition. Billy Graham was the exception and many young men modelled themselves on him. Norman Barnes, founder of Links International, a development agency in the UK, admits practising in front of a mirror with a large black Bible in one hand and the other raised with pointing finger as he shouted, "the Bible says . . ." with a strong American accent.

The words "prophet" and "apostle" were never mentioned except when whispered in hallowed tones of mighty men of God who had long since departed. It is understandable that when some of us, who were being blessed by the Holy Spirit, began to speak about the restoration of these ministries, we were greeted with derision.

Inspired by the simplicity of the church in scripture and concerned about the complexities and divisions in the church today, we longed for something different. We saw that New Testament leadership was not to do with hierarchy or position but with relationships, trust and recognition. It was always plural and invariably functioned in a team context, even among apostles.

Apostles at last!

In the early seventies my booklet *First Apostles, Last Apostles* caused no small stir and achieved notoriety in the Christian press. By this time, the church that my wife and I had started in our home had grown and other groups around the country felt the need of relationships. Networks began to emerge. My little booklet was taken and reprinted in the USA, South America and possibly elsewhere. It touched a nerve in many who were hungry to see an expression of church which more closely resembled that of the Acts of the Apostles.

Today, many believe apostles and prophets are vital to the growth and welfare of the church worldwide. Peter Wagner, author and researcher on church trends, sees a clear link between church growth and the restoration of apostolic ministry. In a talk given in the UK in 1998 he made the following comment:

> I am quite sure we are now seeing the most radical change in the way of "doing church" since the Protestant Reformation. I believe that the change we are seeing now is a *more* radical change than the Protestant Reformation. The most radical change in the Protestant Reformation was a change in theology and that is not a part of what we're seeing now. We are still rooted in the theology of the Reformation – the authority of scripture, the priesthood of all believers, justification by faith. These are the theological bedrocks that were established in the Reformation and they are continuing now. But you take the churches immediately following the Reformation in Europe, the average attender in those churches didn't do very much differently, the life of the church was much the same as it was in the Catholic church . . . What you are seeing now, the restoration of apostles, is the most radical of all changes!

He went on to describe how new apostolic leaders are "doing church" and producing the most exciting period of church growth in history. My conviction is that behind the visible church, which is thrilling enough, there is a far greater invisible church about to emerge. In the USA, Europe and other parts of the world I believe there is an underground movement of disenfranchised saints regrouping with renewed hope, ready to overtake and outshine anything we have seen thus far.

City churches, local churches and apostolic teams

The Argentinian revival has produced an understanding of God's heart for city-wide churches, and it's spreading.

Corporate leadership, which transcends denominational allegiances and personal ambition, works together with apostolic ministries. The primary concern is for the health and expansion of the whole church in the city.

This makes sense if we truly believe there is only one church which belongs to Jesus in its entirety. It's interesting that cities were given as rewards to the wise stewards Jesus spoke of in Luke 19, who had been faithful with only a few talents. Is it an indication that the Lord wants to place our cities in the care of faithful stewards? Surely God's desire for cities, ruled by criminals and corrupt men, must be to place them under the oversight of his people of peace and justice.

All people were created for God. We're called to disciple them into salvation and right relationships, redeeming communities to him. Perhaps this is where the parish system originated, but the reality was lost in rigid structures with no heart for mission.

Protestant reaction to the Roman Catholic hierarchy produced the "autonomous local church", which is nowhere found in scripture. Of course, every local church, every individual or team of Christians is directly answerable to God. No one can say, "My elders made me do it!" or "Our apostle compelled us!" But it is our duty to discover God's order for our lives and relationships together. We are to be inter-dependent, just as the tribes of Israel were; just as the parts of a body are reliant on one another.

When Paul wrote, "First of all apostles" (1 Corinthians 12:28) he was establishing a divine order for church, not a democracy, where everyone's opinions are of equal importance, but rather a theocracy where God reigns through respected leaders with proven ministries whose advice is given serious consideration. We discover God's will together and obey him. In this kind of church humility allows the Holy Spirit to work through every joint and ligament in the body (Ephesians 4:16).

It is significant, and seldom noted, that Jesus, the Apostle and High Priest of our confession, (Hebrews 3:1), never planted a local church, but created a mobile, apostolic team. If local church is the purest expression of church, why did Jesus not plant one as a model for future church builders? The answer is simple: local church is the fruit of God-given apostolic leadership and is just one expression of church which must be viewed in the context of cities which are part of one "holy nation" (1 Peter 2:9).

Israel was the Old Testament prototype of the church, a network of tribes, families, households and individuals called out from among the nations to be a tabernacle for God, a witness to his unity and diversity, one body sharing a common life and purpose. When one rejoiced, all rejoiced and when one suffered, everyone shared the pain. Their destiny was to fill the earth with God's presence.

Called and gathered . . .

The word for church in Greek means "that which is called out" and, by inference, "gathered to purpose." The church has been called out from darkness, sin and the evil world system, and gathered to light, holiness and the government of God. So Paul cautioned the Corinthians, "Do not be yoked together with unbelievers . . . come out from them and be separate" (2 Corinthians 6:14–17). This is a process which constantly challenges us to be humble, flexible and open to change.

We are not called to come out of our traditions and church structures, unless these become a hindrance to our obedience to God. But we acknowledge that we are "but a poor reflection" of the reality (1 Corinthians 13:12) and must be prepared to "come out" and forsake any residue of pride and ignorance that remains in us. We must humbly recognize our limitations and partial understanding, and keep open to the Spirit for fresh revelation as to the nature, shape and mission of the church. This attitude will preserve a healthy balance between maintenance and mission and avoid the paralysis which the demands of upkeep bring. The urgent business of running the church must never draw us away from the important business of growing the church.

... to carry on pioneering

Christine and I are well past 60, and our prayer is, "Lord, do not allow us to settle for the comfortable option. Like Joshua and Caleb of old, may we go forward into everything you have reserved for us. May not the loudness of the music, the fury of the dance or the strangeness of the people keep us from your will for our lives. May not the extremes of your Spirit's working offend us, whether they be silence or high praise, laughter or tears." So we keep mixing with apostles and prophets who will help us to keep moving by their exhortations, encouragement and discipline.

Christine is still pioneering today. She always did play a significant part in the leadership of the churches we planted, though she was not always recognized. Now she is clearly functioning in an apostolic role. She was responsible for a small network of churches in Wales and helped launch a Welsh apostolic team. She gives regular input into churches in Norway, inner city London, the south of England, Bristol and the West Country, as well as developing relationships in Thailand, Africa and India. Neither of us has plans or provision for retirement. We'd love to be around for the second coming; otherwise we'd like to die in our boots!

Biblical leadership models

In the New Testament we see major change to the Israel of Old Testament times. Through the reconciliation of the cross the dividing walls of partition are broken down. The Gentile races are invited to share the Abrahamic root so important to the Jews. Now, in Christ there is one nation with many tribes and, in our heavenly Father, all these families of the earth derive their names (Ephesians 3:15). Good news indeed! This is the foundation on which godly leadership teams, be they extra-local apostles, city-wide elderships, tribal heads or parents, will build the community that is to inherit the earth.

The New Testament clearly shows the Greek words for pastor, elder, bishop, overseer and shepherd are interchangeable. It also reveals that this leadership always functioned in a city-wide context. Old Testament elders "sat in the city gate" (Proverbs 31:23), responsible for the smooth running and the safety of the town. When writing his letters, Paul similarly identifies only one leadership in a city, addressing the elders and saints as one body.

At least some of today's models of leadership – for example, a one-man pastor; five elders in a small local church; worse still, an elected "diaconate" which produces a democratic deadlock; or a strong dominating personality – have little to do with God's order for his people.

A democratic system of voting may work well with mature Christians who have open and honest relationships, but most churches which operate in this way have histories of infighting and division or paralysis through fear of disagreement. Equally, a benevolent dictatorship can work if the "dictator" is Spirit-filled. However these models are not likely to produce a plurality of leadership which empowers the people. Things the Lord tolerated in the past when we were moving from ignorance into understanding, will no longer be acceptable. We must rediscover how biblical leadership functions.

However we respond, the "shaking" will do its work. Fresh models of scriptural leadership appropriate to today's needs will emerge. Apostolic input will develop strong city churches with co-operation among leaders across streams and the church will increasingly find herself in the public arena addressing issues of justice, ethics and morality. A questioning generation unwilling to be led by tradition, because that's the way it's always been, will respond and the gaps between genders, generations and groups, and between worship and the work-a-day world, will disappear.

Recognizing and releasing apostles

The question is – how do we recognize and release apostles? There is a short and a lengthy answer. The lengthy answer would be the subject of another book, so the short answer must suffice. In Matthew 7:16, speaking of false prophets, Jesus said, "By their fruit you will recognize them." This principle also applies to genuine ministry. We cannot appoint apostles, nor can we produce them by giving out titles. Prophets and apostles will be recognized by their fruit.

Discover the outcome of apostolic ministry and wherever you see it the apostle will not be far away. Find a majestic building and there will be a great architect behind it; a beautiful painting is the evidence of a skilled artist. Strong churches, reconciled saints, empowered people, co-operating leaders, new churches planted, will be the signs of an apostle, team or an emerging apostolic ministry. They don't just happen! Trouble is, we Christians tend to judge personality before results. You can't write off a painting because you don't like the artist! Who said Paul was a nice guy to know?

When we have recognized apostles, how do we release them? Well, ministry can only function successfully in an atmosphere of respect, honour and submission. If I recognize that someone has a greater, or different, gift than mine, I release them into my situation by humbly yielding to their wisdom and input.

I'm not talking about blind obedience, giving way to control or becoming "yes" people. Rather, we should simply be open to receive from those Jesus has raised up to develop the church in character and power. It shouldn't be difficult. Today there is a growing army of such leaders in all the churches. They are becoming easier to recognize, and the release of their ministry is in our hands.

Apostolic centres

These apostolic people, given by Jesus to equip, inspire and motivate, will often be found in apostolic centres or resource churches. Jerusalem and Antioch provide biblical examples, and we must expect to find such centres as the restoration of church order takes place. Local or rural churches may group around or relate to these centres.

I imagine the original cathedral communities and monastic orders were intended to be such places of prayer and ministry where vision, teaching, care and oversight were dispensed. Those who receive from these centres will, in turn, give their support, releasing the ministries to pioneer in other geographical areas and spheres of influence. In this way healthy growth and expansion will take place.

Roger Ellis, founder of "Fusion" (a new initiative to encourage cells in universities) identifies three characteristics of apostolic centres and people. They will first act as *catalysts* to encourage fresh thinking and radical new ways to achieve our God-given mission to reach all peoples. Secondly, they will nurture *co-operation* among all who share a heart to complete this task, and thirdly, they will *conspire* together, exchanging dreams and visions to ensure they become reality.

I add a fourth characteristic – *care*. I understand Roger's reluctance to include this, lest we get bogged down in maintenance. Nevertheless, we must look after what God has entrusted to us lest valuable resources in our churches are lost or remain locked up.

Caring hands

Drawing from the analogy of the body, if Christ is the head then the hands are the servant ministries which care for the body. My visual imagery may not appeal to some, but it makes a point, it's fun and you'll remember it! Think of the hand with its four fingers and one thumb as representing the five ministries of Ephesians 4, apostle, prophet, evangelist, pastor and teacher. The thumb is the apostle, similar in function to the fingers but able to move apart from them. It is stronger and works well with any one finger or combination.

The pointing, index finger is the prophet. He or she exhorts, admonishes and encourages us by pointing to the glories to come and to sin in our lives and relationships. The prophet is not an arrogant wagging finger, for the message has been tried and tested within his or her life and experience. Three other fingers point back as a reminder of the prophet's own frailty. They do not simply deliver a message but participate by sharing its blessings and heeding its warnings. The prophet also beckons, calling us to a higher and deeper relationship with Jesus.

The middle finger represents the evangelist. It is robust and, unless misshapen, it is the digit which can reach out further than its partners. Mission cannot be tagged on to our agendas;

it *is* the agenda and must be at the heart of all servant leadership.

The third finger is the pastor. In most cultures it is the ring finger, speaking of covenant and marriage. Pastors watch over the church, preparing her for marriage to Jesus; mature, blameless, without spot or wrinkle, a fitting bride for our king. They are not sentimental or mollycoddling, but firm and loving, demonstrating the qualities of commitment, care and discipline so needed in all our lives to make us armies as opposed to the hospitals so many churches have become.

Finally, the smallest digit is the teacher. The pastor and the teacher are closely related. Like the two fingers representing them they are often unable to move alone; they strongly influence one another. When one moves the other is drawn along, but the teacher is not simply an extension of the pastor. The little finger is unique, for it can penetrate the ear most deeply, ensuring that we hear the voice of God!

A hand with missing fingers is incomplete and lacks some ability. To serve the body we need two hands, with all fingers and thumbs working together in harmony. The hands are not the body, and they are certainly not the head. Controlled by the head, the hands are willing slaves to the whole body.

Handy functions

Hands perform many functions; they wash, dress and feed the body. They are lifted in worship, come together in supplication and indicate the body's yieldedness to God. They are opened to receive from the Lord and they reach out with his provisions for a needy world. They represent the heart and soul of the body with their expressions of welcome peace and healing which unite, or violence and anger which repel.

We are all called to bless one another through the laying on of hands (1 Timothy 4:14). Not suddenly (5:22), but with prayer and consideration, for this is not mere symbolism – we actually impart the Holy Spirit, endorse and empower one another in this way. Churches like Antioch, with their rich mix of culture, ministry and experience, release the cream of its leadership as "hands," in apostolic service to care for other parts of the body. Truly we are fearfully and wonderfully made.

CHAPTER 10

MOVERS AND SHAKERS

For heaven's sake go . . .

"Movers and shakers" well describes the apostles and prophets. We have seen that the church was mobile before it was residential, and was threatening before it became acceptable. Jesus' priority was to invest his prime time into 12 men and a travelling group, which radically broke with tradition by including women.

Frequently it was women who displayed the qualities Jesus was seeking to instill. Their passion, sacrifice, faithfulness, understanding and response are the subjects of many Bible stories. Much of Jesus' teaching was in the temple court of the women, which is obvious from the narrative. The widow making her offering during Jesus' lengthy discourse in Luke 20 and 21 could only have been there. This offended the rabbis, who would rather have buried the scriptures in a cesspit than teach them to a woman.

So Jesus was a mover and shaker; he would not be limited by religious or political forces and challenged the Jewish and Roman traditions. He also ensured that those who carried on the work of the kingdom would follow fearlessly in his footsteps.

The simplest word which expresses the apostolic vocation is "go." "Go in my place; go with my authority; go in my name; go into all the world; go and preach the gospel to all people; go and make disciples of all nations." This was Jesus' commission to his team after $3^1/_2$ years of on-the-job training. However, the one who said "go," first said "come" – another word related to movement – and response to this call was costly. They forsook all to follow Jesus. He loved them, healed them, equipped them and sent them out.

. . . but first come!

How can we leaders commission the church to "go," unless we have "come" alongside Jesus and experienced his commitment, healing and discipleship ourselves? How can God's people take the apostolic mantle unless they taste the same kind of love, care and discipline Jesus offered? The Greek for apostleship is "apostole." "Apo" is translated in different ways but most commonly "from," "of" or "out of," literally "away from"; "stole," is a long robe or "garment of significance."[1]

I'm aware the true meaning of a word lies in its current usage. However, this root meaning is in harmony with what the New Testament reveals about apostleship. If the ministry is a gift of the ascended Christ, anointed by the Spirit, it comes "from" the covering of a "garment of significance." The mantle of Elijah rested on Elisha (2 Kings 2:13–14), so the mantle of Jesus rests on those he sends, and their disciples too. The "garment of significance" covers the whole body. In this way Jesus' ministry achieves maximum exposure through every member – an apostolic church.

Shaken and stirred

Watching Jesus we become aware of the commotion and excitement that surrounded him. "Where is he going now?" "What
will he do next?" Heaving crowds, screaming demons, dancing
cripples, silent hypocrites, astounding words kept everyone on
their toes, straining to see what was coming. Jerusalem was
shaken – a stark contrast to the predictability of our churches
and activity. We know exactly where we'll be and what we'll be
doing. The sanctified hours of 11am and 6:30pm come and go
with the precision of a metronome. The chant drones in our
ears, "As it was in the beginning, is now and ever shall be church
without change. Amen."

Looking at the noticeboard of one church, I did see a hint
of excitement. "DIVINE WORSHIP (is there any other kind?)
11am and 6:30pm – ALL WELCOME – BEWARE OF FALLING
MASONRY!" Being hit by a gargoyle might put you out of your
misery, but it could never have happened in the early church –
they had no buildings. Actually, many new churches, proud
that they have no plant or liturgy, are not much better. They've
just swapped the "hymn/prayer sandwich" for the
"chorus/picture burger." After the death and burial of Jesus the
early church was paralyzed with fear, but when the Holy Spirit
fell they were immediately transformed into dynamic movers
and shakers.

The new wine was poured out in the upper room "bar"; they
were well and truly drunk with the Spirit. The heavenly land-
lord called, "Time, ladies and gentlemen, please!" and thrust
them out into the busy market at nine in the morning.
Overwhelmed by the Spirit, intimidation and fear melted away.
Those who had been moved and shaken became the movers and
shakers, and Jerusalem quaked. Hell was also shaken and in
one day 3,000 souls were released from death into life.

The passion persists . . .

A pattern was established. Moving and shaking continued in prayer gatherings and prison cells. Ordinary saints, filled with the Spirit who empowered Jesus, were bold in the face of opposition and persecution. Wide-eyed jailers fell under conviction, pleading for forgiveness. Cities were stirred as the good news spread like wildfire through the teaching of the apostles and the testimony of ordinary people who believed. Soon the whole world seemed to be buzzing. Can we believe that anything less will meet today's colossal needs?

At times the flame burned low but courageous women and men carried the torch from one generation to the next. In *2000 Years of Charismatic Christianity* Eddie Hyatt traces this stream of the Spirit through the Ante-Nicene church into monasticism and on to the Reformation. From here he shows how it gathered momentum with Anabaptists, Quakers and Moravians. In turn these movements gave rise to the "Great Awakenings" of the 18th and 19th centuries.

. . . and is passed on . . .

In the UK in 1865 William Booth, a Methodist, founded the Salvation Army. He saw the plight of homeless children in London's East End and realized the gospel was inadequate unless linked to social concern. My family on both my sides were involved in the earliest days, my grandfather being Lt. Col. John Noble.

I was close to my grandmother, who was a soldier in Booth's days. She told stories of clashes with the "Skeleton Army," which came out in opposition whenever Booth's soldiers marched. Their symbol, the skull and crossbones, was paraded on a menacing black flag. Stones and bottles were hurled, but the angry threats did not deter.

The soldiers prayed and sang for hours until the Spirit came. Some would fall to the ground in "glory fits," others made strange unrecognizable sounds we now know as speaking in tongues. Filled with boldness, after marching round the hall with shouts of praise and banging drums, some brave soldier would grasp the flag and lead the others into the night and on to the pub or bar to "rescue the perishing."

Dragging or carrying the drunks back to the meeting place, the soldiers would preach until their audience was sober. A bench became the "mercy seat," where many a rogue wept his way to the cross. The leaders were often brave young women who preached and carried responsibility for the corps. Booth, when confronted by rowdy drunks, would call Evangeline, his daughter, to face the crowd. She was a great evangelist and such was the power of her words that silence fell and soon the trouble-makers were weeping their way to Jesus.

In the open air the seekers knelt beside the big drum, smitten with their sin and crying to God for mercy. The soldiers would pray until revelation came. Sometimes it was hours before the joyful shout went up, "I've seen the light!" Frequently, these converts were immediately radically changed. Filled with a different Spirit, they would return to the very same pub to give testimony to the great things God had done and call their friends to Christ.

Booth has been called "the general next to God." However, we must also see him and the warriors who served him, as apostles, men and women "going forth" with the "mantle of significance." They were 19th century apostles and prophets, whose faith and courage took the gospel into almost every nation. Incidentally, it was my grandmother and mother who prayed for me during my days of backsliding. Sadly, grandma did not live to see me come back to the Lord, but she will have her reward.

. . . to the next generation

When as a young married man I was restored, I was soon
inspired by the dynamic church of the Acts. Unable to relate to
what I saw in the existing church, I began to seek God for something new. We prayed for revival in nights and half-nights of
prayer. Some great old saints who shared those meetings in the
early sixties had first-hand experience of the Pentecostal pioneers. They'd seen the fires sparked by the Welsh revival and the
Azusa Street revival in the early 1900s. From these humble
beginnings almost half-a-billion Pentecostal and Charismatic
Christians can trace their roots.

I learned of the Jeffreys brothers, Smith Wigglesworth, Willie
Burton and many others in Britain; of Frank Bartleman,
William Seymour, Charles Price and the Latter Rain movement
in the USA. Mighty miracles of healing, dead bodies raised to
life, thousands saved and filled with the Holy Spirit were the
order of the day.

The press loved or hated them, but they were always good
for a story. Just before the First World War, in July 1914,
Stephen Jeffreys was preaching in Llanelli, Wales. A vision of
the suffering Lamb of God appeared on the wall behind him.
It remained there for hours while queues of people filed
through the church. Many felt it was a warning of what was to
come in that horrific conflict and also a reminder of God's love
for lost humanity.

Critical mass

No one can deny these pioneers moved in the passion and
power of Jesus under an apostolic "mantle of significance."
They made the way for today's renewals which burn so brightly
in many parts of the world. However, if we are to increase

effectiveness and speed the preaching of the gospel to all people we must reach "critical mass."

"Critical mass" is the minimum amount of fissile material needed to maintain a nuclear chain reaction. It is an exact balance between neutrons generated and those absorbed. If there is more than a "critical mass" there is an uncontrolled explosion. In a nuclear generator control rods are used to maintain the "just critical" condition. In the spiritual realm, the Holy Spirit is generating a great deal of activity. Soon this activity will produce "critical mass" in the divine power station of the church. Apostolic ministries are control rods and the Lord is putting them in place to ensure that power is controlled and gets where it is needed.

Multiplication of apostles

There are many known ministries we can point to as apostolic gifts to the body of Christ and more unknown. Let me remind you of a few modern examples. Jackie Pullinger with her work amongst the addicts of Hong Kong has had a profound effect on the church worldwide. John and Carol Arnott at Toronto Airport Vineyard Church have positively reshaped the experience of multitudes of Christians from all denominations and all corners of the globe. Sandy Millar and Nicky Gumbel from Holy Trinity Brompton in London's West End, as apostolic evangelists have given us "Alpha" and thousands have been drawn to Jesus. Ed Silvoso and the Argentinian revivalists are helping us rediscover how to take cities for God.

The "March for Jesus" team of Lynn Green, a director of YWAM, Roger Forster, leader of the Ichthus Fellowship in London, Gerald Coates, leader of the Pioneer Network and Graham Kendrick, songwriter and worship leader, have helped millions from almost every nation take their worship on to the streets. John Presdee, part of that vision, has led prayer marches in many countries over thousands of miles. He also supported Lynn Green's reconciliation walk over the original Crusade route, helping heal old wounds among Muslims, Christians and Jews.

Myles Munroe, a black leader in the Bahamas, has risen from obscurity to distinction by his dedication and the power of the Holy Spirit. Now he moves at the highest levels in business, politics and the church, giving advice on financial and racial issues, as well as encouraging thousands of black and white Christians to find their identity and destiny in Jesus.

Watchman Nee, Aimée Semple McPherson, Billy Graham, Ralph Martin, Carlos Anacondia, Paul Raj, Corrie ten Boom, Jim Packer, David Yonggi Cho, Bill Brightman, Cindy Jacobs, George Verwer, Jean Darnall, John Wimber, Tom Forrest, Omar Cabrera, Gladys Aylward, John Stott, Ezekiel Gutu, Derek Prince . . . All these and many, many more unsung heroines and heroes have served the church as apostolic and prophetic movers and shakers in a multiplicity of different ways.

Seeing we are surrounded by this ever-increasing cloud of witnesses, let us follow their example and look to Jesus the captain of this great and growing army. Let us "go forth" as one body, under "the mantle of significance" to shake the foundations of society and move the people to recognize their need of Jesus, Messiah.

Notes

1. αποστελλω (apostellō) means 'I send' or 'I dispatch'.

CHAPTER 11

THE NEHEMIAH PRINCIPLE
AND THE NEW JERUSALEM

Nehemiah, apostle of restoration

Although apostles were not so labelled in the Old Testament, the ministry is modelled there. Nehemiah wonderfully expresses the essence and prophetic character of apostolic calling. He led the nation in rebuilding God's city and his story provides insights into the nature of today's task. He was the Old Testament apostle of restoration and demonstrated the importance of vision and intercession working hand in hand.

Nehemiah was not just a man with a mission; he was obsessed with a passion to see Jerusalem rebuilt and flourishing again. Shattered by the devastation, he lived for nothing other than the peace and welfare of the city. He risked his life as cupbearer to obtain the king's blessing and resources to raise the walls and hang the gates so his people could dwell together in peace and safety once more. In his position, to enter the king's presence in sadness was certain death, but Nehemiah found favour and was granted his petition. So began this remarkable story of restoration.

Identifying with the need

Psalm 100 exhorts us to "shout for joy to the Lord," to "come before him with joyful songs," to "enter his gates with thanksgiving." There's no reason to be miserable in God's presence; he has given us "all things richly to enjoy." However, when we see his gates burned and his courts under heaps of rubble, it is time for tears, and tears move our King. His hand will provide all we need to begin the work and his commission will give us authority to overrule all opposition and build.

As one would expect of a wise master-builder, Nehemiah gathered friends and assessed the damage. Far from deterring him, the enormity of the job spurred him on. "Jerusalem lies in ruins and its gates are burned," he cried, "Come let us rebuild . . . we will no longer be in disgrace." He accepted blame for the condition of the city, though he was not responsible for its collapse. We too should identify with the sins of our nation or people and acknowledge past failures.

Identificational repentance?

Before proceeding I must briefly address a currently important issue – "identificational repentance." In time, a theology will emerge to give biblical justification for what is happening in the realm of reconciliation. In this respect Chris Seaton of Peaceworks has written a helpful paper – "Identificational Repentance – Towards a Definition?" It was inspired by a Theological Round Table held at Spurgeon's Bible College in London, England, in February 2000. Despite the inevitable hype and optimism which surround new blessing, deep chasms of historic division are being healed – on occasions instantly – as the Holy Spirit breaks open the hearts of tribes and nations that have been at odds for centuries.

Some prefer the term "representational" or "substitutional repentance," that is, standing in on behalf of others to convey remorse for past sins of their people or group. Even more helpful is "representational" or "substitutional identification," which fits my understanding of scripture calling us to "weep with those who weep." This must involve some form of identificational bridge between the victim and perpetrator, if not actual repentance. These are not biblical phrases, but they do seem to convey the spirit of what scripture teaches. Personally, it has been a privilege to become a point of release in this way for hurting people on a number of occasions with amazing results as the barriers of years came tumbling down.

One of the most moving moments of my life occurred while I was ministering in a church in the Transkei, South Africa. At the end of my time there Iris Mniki, wife of the leader, asked me to stand before the entirely black, Xhosa congregation. God had spoken to her and she was not about to glorify me, a white man, but was demonstrating that the pain and hurt inflicted upon them by people of my colour was forgiven. The congregation fully received me into their midst as an apostle of God.

Iris then knelt down and washed my feet with her copious tears. I was utterly broken, as were that whole congregation. After some time, I asked permission to respond. Encouraging Iris to stand, I got down and washed her feet with my tears. It was not difficult for me to do in that broken state. The place was electric; demons of suspicion and pain fled that room never to return.

Following this experience, I am working more closely with these precious people and other South African leaders. Together we had the joy of meeting and praying for Peter Marais, mayor of Cape Town. This fine outspoken Christian man wept as this motley crew of black, mixed race and white church leaders gave him their united backing for the difficult and lonely task God had entrusted to him.

Seeing through the victim's eyes

It is hard to feel remorse for things that happened long ago, things you were totally unaware of and remote from. But try to see from the perspective of the victim who has been wronged or abused. Imagine it was your brother or close family member who was guilty of violence or rape and you find yourself in the same circle as the injured person. It would surely be crass and insensitive to pass over their feelings of pain towards you as a relation with, "I'm sorry, it was nothing to do with me."

Surely, in such circumstances, we would identify and allow ourselves to become the point of release for the anger and pain, a substitute so that reconciliation could take place. As with Nehemiah, it starts with God. Nehemiah humbled himself and became the focus for reconciliation. Jesus did it too when he stood in and dealt with our sin at Calvary. Now he calls us to take up our cross and follow his example.

A function of priesthood

Beyond the need for us to do this as individuals, the Lord calls us corporately, as his representatives in the world, to do the same. Martin Scott says in "Prophetic Intercession," some unpublished notes:

> A belief in the church as a priesthood . . . goes beyond the reformational understanding of the priesthood of all believers – implying that we have direct access to the Father as an individual. It is the understanding that the church itself is called to be a priestly nation on behalf of the nations. This flows from the understanding of the call for Israel to be a light to the nations, to be the means of salvation coming to the Gentiles. So the church as holy nation, royal priesthood, is to carry the same call. The priestly ministry is one of reconciliation – of standing between two alienated parties and

bringing them together; it is one of carrying some measure of guilt on behalf of others.

Another helpful contribution here in Britain is Brian Mills' and Roger Mitchell's *Sins of the Fathers* (Sovereign World). The book outlines their journey and experiences in many parts of the world, and examines Britain's history of failure in many nations. In his introduction John Dawson, founder of "International Reconciliation Coalition," says, "We of other nations sometimes reflexively associate England with arrogance . . ." He points out that the authors have done much to change that view. What a wonderful opportunity for we English to reverse the bad effects of our past through priestly acts of repentance, intercession and reconciliation.

New Testament apostles

The New Covenant marked a significant change in emphasis. God's heart to see a prophetic people functioning in a priestly role means that old-style individual authoritarian prophetic figures give way to a new kind of oversight, which releases the people to become the ministry.

New Testament leadership functioned in plurality and mutual submission, the final authority in the gathered church. Apostles and prophets demonstrated mutuality and submission, which also exists in the Godhead. Sent by God, released and endorsed by the church, they made themselves accountable (not subservient) in the locality and to extra-local ministries. The body was bound together in truth and loving relationships. No longer can independent, "lone-ranger" itinerants roam the world foisting themselves on unwary churches and causing all kinds of damage and hurt.

Genuine apostles identify with the needs of God's people.

They will be answerable to God for the sorry state of the church and will work humbly with all who share their concerns. Wisdom and perseverance are inherent in the ministry and the ability to continue steadfast in the face of persecution and opposition will see them through.

When confronted with sin and chaos in Corinth, Paul embraced the people before he rebuked them, saying, "you are the seal of my apostleship in the Lord" (1 Corinthians 9:2). Drunkenness, greed, litigation, wrong doctrine, misuse of gifts and immorality were not enough to dissuade him from being involved and identifying. He saw only precious stones that could be built into the temple of his God. Had I been asked if I had anything to do with such a church, I guess I might have replied with a distant look, "Well, I did visit once, but it was a long time ago!"

Co-operation – key to success

The work began under the watchful eye of Nehemiah, but could only be carried out by those who could produce proof of their Jewishness. We would have expected slaves, servants or outside labourers to take on this heavy work. However, so great was the privilege and responsibility that only tribal members could participate. Each family had their place and so the walls and gates were simultaneously rebuilt.

With the opposition they faced and the intensity of the work (the walls took only 52 days to complete) they could not have finished without solidarity, dedication and strong leadership. Today missiologists are convinced that the worldwide church has more than enough resources to evangelize the nations. It is only lack of co-operation among Christians that holds us back. Like Nehemiah, apostolic ministry will prod and provoke us to give our time, possessions and abilities to serve God's objectives.

We must join with Jesus in the prayer he prayed before going to the cross – "Father . . . may they be brought to complete unity to let the world know that you sent me" (John 17:23). This is why he died, why he shares his glory with his church. Apostolic and prophetic people will be consumed with a longing to see God's people united in purpose and effort to show the world their Saviour. "Behold, the Lamb of God!" will be their cry, not now on a Roman cross, but alive and well in his people. The manifestation of Jesus to a generation in his "many-membered" body will precede his second coming in his physical body as visible head of the church.

During the final supper our Lord ate with his disciples, he broke bread and poured wine. Giving them the elements identified as his body and his blood, he called them to partake in remembrance of him. In 1 Corinthians, Paul reminds us of this and warns about failing to recognize the body of the Lord when we share together. He points out this is one reason why weakness and sickness exists among Christians (1 Corinthians 11:30).

It is interesting that the English word "re-member" has a more significant meaning than simply "being mindful." "Remembering" means putting back together a body that has been torn apart. Reconciliation should be central to our common meals where heaven and earth sit with us looking on at every table in home or gathered church.

1 Corinthians says much about the unity of God's people. In chapter 1 verse 10, Paul's burden comes through, "I appeal to you, brothers, in the name of our Lord Jesus Christ, that all of you agree with one another so that there may be no divisions among you . . ." This theme continues through the book, revealing how Paul shared Jesus' concern for harmony in the church. Nehemiah's success in uniting and mobilizing just a remnant of the nation had a sobering effect on his enemies: 'all the surrounding nations were afraid and lost their self-confidence' (Nehemiah 6:16).

Local churches and networks which are isolated or independent are vulnerable to the enemy and to human frailties. These devastate, divide and destroy. Joined-up walls provide protection, and a vital communication link with all parts of the city. Anointed, servant leadership in the gates, means watchmen are ready to act to preserve the wellbeing of all who live within the city of peace.

Lessons to be learned

There are other lessons for us in Nehemiah's story. First, he had a clear understanding of what needed to be done. He had seen the plans and knew how to organize the workforce. Second, he had the anointing to bring discipline and maintain the morale through hardships and threats. Third, he had the resolve to remain focused when enemies tried to distract him. He refused to be drawn away from his task. Fourth, he instilled courage in the hearts of his people. Fifth, he put great store in prayer and the faithfulness of God's word. He believed that God fulfills his promises.

Nehemiah's example shows us the qualities we expect to find in apostolic teams today. The skills which enabled him to raise Jerusalem up from heaps of rubble are exactly those we require to bring order in today's church. Never has there been a more urgent need for Nehemiah's leadership to bring courage, direction and purpose to God's work. As evil threatens to engulf the world, blinding its people, we need "the city set on the hill whose light cannot be hid."

The walls completed, the gates hung, Nehemiah made his leadership appointments. Gatekeepers, singers and priests were put in place. A church united and working together across a town will have clear oversight, strong worship and solid pastoral ministries. The reason many city-wide church initiatives, which looked so promising, did not evolve from occasional evangelism or celebration into full-blooded co-operation, has been the lack of godly authority. In the growing number of centres around the world where there has been a measure of success, it is the result of prayer and proven apostolic involvement.

Walls and gates

If the rebuilt walls represent repaired relationships among saints, then the imagery of the gates speaks of security. The elders sat in the city gates overseeing what was coming in and going out. Nehemiah gave instructions that the gates were not to be opened for traffic till the sun was high. This meant, in the light of day, the inspection of goods and of those who were seeking entrance to the city was relatively easy.

Many an unscrupulous tradesman would try to smuggle in poor quality or illegal goods, and enemy spies were always looking for ways into the city. There were 11 gates giving access and one, the Dung Gate, through which rubbish was carried out to the tip. If there was no quality control at the 11 entry points, there would be a great deal of activity going on at the exit!

The speaking gates . . .

The gates, 12 in all, speak about the kind of the city we are occupying. Twelve is the biblical number of government. Twelve patriarchs, Jacob's sons, were the founding government of the Old Covenant. Twelve disciples of Jesus provided a new spiritual order for the church.

In Revelation 21 we see the New Jerusalem, the Holy City, coming down to earth from heaven. It has 12 gates closely linked to Israel's roots with the names of the tribes and the 12 apostles inscribed on the foundations of the walls. Thus the city is firmly rooted in the government of the God of both old and new covenants.

I referred to the Dung Gate as the place of cleansing: the other 11 gates are also full of symbolic meaning. The Valley Gate speaks of testing, humility and repentance; the Fountain Gate calls to mind the cleansing power of Jesus' blood. The Sheep Gate reminds us of the pastoral relationship of Jesus and the Fish Gate of our mission to disciple the nations. Jeshanah or the Old Gate points back to our historic roots and the "Ancient of Days," through whom we have eternal life.

The Water Gate is symbolic of the Holy Spirit and his provision for life and the Horse Gate speaks of power for service. The East Gate assures that, as the sun rises, so our king is coming back. Miphkad, the Inspection or Registry Gate, is a reminder that the Great Recorder has our names written in his book of life, while the Ephraim Gate promises fruitfulness as our inheritance in Christ.

Finally the Prison Gate, not mentioned until Nehemiah 12:39, warns us of the reality of hell. Incidentally, the Prison or Guard Gate is the only gate not in need of repair. This is the place where so many are held captive. It is our prerogative as the church to take the keys so the gates of hell will yield, allowing the captives to go free as they respond to Jesus.

. . . of the New Jerusalem

What a city! The one our father Abraham looked for, whose maker and builder is God (Hebrews 11:10). This city with foundations in Christ and his apostles can never be shaken or moved. A place where there is "no more death or mourning or crying or pain, for the old order has passed away." There is no night there, nor any need of light, for the lamb, the light of the world, is in the midst. Like a jasper it's a very precious jewel, clear as crystal (Revelation 21:1 – 22:6).

The gates are 12 pearls and the street is pure gold, like transparent glass. There is no temple because the Lord God Almighty and the Lamb are its temple and the nations will walk in the light. The gates will never be shut and nothing impure will enter. The glory and honour of the nations will be brought into it and, sisters and brothers, to you who hold the name of Jesus dear, this city of Shalom, of God's abiding peace, is us!

CHAPTER 12

WHERE HAVE ALL THE FATHERS GONE?

The father famine

Fathering is a dying practice. Some say that in the West there is a lack of fathers, but my wife and I travel in many countries and we see it is a global problem. In Africa Christine has had wives of Christian leaders come secretly to ask for prayer as their husbands were guilty of multiple sexual relationships. And that is not uncommon in some countries of the Continent. In other places, poorer and rural areas, there is still a strong sense of family or community, but men dominate and are often selfish.

In India we have walked through miles of planted fields and jungle to reach remote villages. Always we were treated like royalty, but even among these lovely, simple people men ate first, then children and finally, if there was any food left, the women ate.

In one village Christine paid for a feast, insisting the men served the women and children. After a few women received food she asked why they had no meat, only rice on their leaf plates. The sheepish reply from the elders who served the meal was they were worried there would be none left for them!

Needless to say, Christine ministered discipline. The women got meat, much to their amusement and delight.

In the West marriage and family are regarded as outmoded, remnants of a bygone era, and we are reaping the results in a hurting generation damaged, in the main, by absentee fathers. In the church, even mature Christians seem to have little concept of fatherhood, when we should be nurturing the young and those new to faith, acting as role models and advisors. Instead we alienate them by clinging to old forms of worship and practices more to do with personal preference than reaching the marginalized. So much for maturity!

Founding fathers

Fatherhood is a foundation of our faith. It is central to life and is strongly linked to apostolic, prophetic and pastoral leadership in scripture. In Romans, Paul refers to Abraham as "the father of all who believe" (4:11) and God's promise was he would be "the father of many nations" (Genesis 17:3). Thus fatherhood is a fundamental theme throughout the Bible.

Elisha calls his master Elijah "My father! My father," as he is caught up to heaven (2 Kings 2:12). We have seen how Nehemiah fathered a nation from ruin to restoration. Jesus is identified as the "Everlasting Father," (Isaiah 9:6) and pointed out to his bemused disciple Philip, "Anyone who has seen me has seen the Father" (John 14:9). He also taught us to recognize God as Father and to address him as such when we pray, (Matthew 6:9).

The theme continues through the New Testament. In Acts 7:2 fatherhood is linked to leadership when the Sanhedrin are referred to as "fathers." In 1 Corinthians 4:15–16, Paul describes himself as a father to underline the uniqueness of his ministry to the church there. John, in his first epistle, emphasizes the importance of fathers in the Christian community. Elsewhere there are constant reminders of the fatherly nature of God as the ultimate prototype for us all.

New Age deception

In this new "age of Aquarius" gurus tell us that humanity is coming of age. Emerging from the darkness and ignorance of "Pisces," the era of the fish, we are to break free from oppressive paternalism and the old patriarchal society to take control of our destiny. True, there are many chauvinistic elements of our culture that we would be well rid of. Male dominance, legalism, cruelty to women and children and the underprivileged, are wrong, but Luciferian New Age philosophy leads to rebellion and the collapse of society.

We cannot go back, because the "good old days" never existed. The way forward is to grasp the biblical concept of fatherhood. The last verse of the Old Testament, and a signpost, pointing towards the New, speaks of Elijah coming to "turn the hearts of the fathers to their children and the hearts of the children to their fathers" (Malachi 4:6).

The delicate balance

I referred to transcendence and immanence or awe and familiarity in an earlier chapter. Let me say again, we will never understand Father God unless we know something of the paradox of these contrasting characteristics. The Great Creator, All Powerful One to be feared and revered is also Abba Daddy, who loves to be intimate with his children. This tension of respect and affection should be welcomed in our relationships with our natural and spiritual fathers – it's healthy!

As we model God's fatherhood in our families and churches,

we must maintain that delicate balance. Leaders should conduct themselves in a way which expresses genuine friendship and affection, whilst maintaining the right to bring correction in love. Time, experience, and the Spirit can teach us this. My father died when I was 16 and the church then was in a desperate state. As a leader in my twenties I had to learn on the job, for we had few we could look to as fathers. I felt like an elder brother left to lead a family whose parents had been taken away. It was tough.

Nevertheless, I praise God for the struggles for now, after more than 40 years of ministry I am most frequently referred to as a "father." I feel humbled by this and incredibly thankful to God that it is so. However, all is relative and I'm aware that my achievements are exaggerated in a culture where good fathers are the exception. It's not difficult to shine in a subject where there are few other students.

Why fatherhood and not parenthood?

I admit, I struggled with this emphasis on fatherhood. Not because it is unbiblical. My concern is that men tend to turn any attention they receive into an excuse to feed their feelings of superiority. The reason why, after the fall, the Lord placed the primary responsibility for the partnership on Adam, was because of his efforts to pass the buck and put the blame on God and the woman, not because he was better equipped or superior. Why, even the serpent was not implicated by Adam: "The *woman* you put here with me – *she* gave me some fruit . . ." (Genesis 3:12), he whined, avoiding the reality of his own disobedience. The woman, on the other hand, accepting she had been deceived by the devil, implicated neither God nor Adam. The Lord counterbalanced the male inclination to "opt out" with an obligation to provide and oversee, and the female tendency to "opt in" with a duty to yield and receive.

By removing the curse of the Fall on the cross, Jesus reversed the inevitable battling of the sexes to make perfect gender harmony and order possible. Major responsibility rests on he who was primarily to blame – man! Thus Jesus, "The Man," led the way to paradise restored by laying down his life. He left us a pattern of humility and sacrifice for us all to follow. This makes good husbands and fathers!

The benefits of fatherhood

Benefits of fatherhood are obvious as we watch the difference in behaviour between children with a secure family environment and those without. However, it's not just children who are affected by the lack of fathers. Fewer and fewer people can sustain meaningful relationships and so live in isolation. The accompanying problems of loneliness, depression, poverty and mental torture are all around. The housing shortage in the UK is not to do with population growth but the numbers of people who need to live alone to avoid the pressures of fractured relationships. So, to the benefits –

Identity

Ephesians 3:14–15 tells us that it is ". . . the Father, from whom his whole family in heaven and on earth derives its name . . ." The Hebrew word "ab" means "ancestor" and implies an historic relationship with continuity. Israel with 12 founding fathers and the church with 12 apostles provide us with a context in which every earthly family has a place and a destiny.

Belonging and having roots is important for us all as individuals, families and peoples. This enabled the Jewish community to survive dispersion and persecution for thousands of years. We should honour our roots, both recent and historic, physical and spiritual. New and independent churches have not been good in this and have paid the price. There is little sense of continuity, no rights of passage and hardly any understanding of our heritage.

The fifth commandment carries with it the promise of longevity in the land (Exodus 20:12). Sadly, many today do not even know their biological parents and sense no need of spiritual ones. They have no identity, no one to respect. So, fathers must seek out the orphans inside and outside the church, and begin the process of caring and mentoring them. Then we will experience the stability the command promises.

Security

"Ab," mentioned above, can also be translated as "source," while the Greek "pater" means "nourisher, protector and upholder." The Aramaic, "Abba" means "daddy," and is among a child's first words of recognition or a cry for help. This provides a picture of fatherhood as a familiar fountain from which flow security, safety and sustenance.

The Catholic theologian Brennan Manning is convinced that Jesus constantly used the Aramaic "Abba" or "Daddy" when addressing his Father, since it was his natural tongue. He believes the truth of this was lost as scripture was recorded in Greek. This means that when Jesus taught his disciples to pray "our Father," he encouraged them to call on "Abba," fostering trust and intimacy as a base from which to make their requests.

The security a good father provides brings about an environment of peace and wellbeing in which children flourish. Psalm 23 is loved because it beautifully describes our heavenly Father's care. It contains all elements of fatherhood and is a revealing insight into the depth of David's experience. "The Lord is *my* shepherd" speaks of a personal relationship giving him identity. "I shall not be in want," is a statement of absolute confidence in Father's provision. "Green pastures" and "quiet waters" describe the deep peace in Daddy's presence, while "paths of righteousness" speak of discipline and truth. There is total commitment, even through suffering and death, with provision right under the enemy's nose. Finally, the Father's house is eternal and unassailable and I am forever welcome.

Encouragement

Encouragement is needed everywhere these days. God knows there's enough of the other stuff around. Criticism and cynicism thrive in all areas of society. The media constantly scrutinize anyone in public life from celebrity to politician and monarch. How infrequently we hear the words, "well done!" The Greek "parakaleo" – "called alongside," in the Authorized Version is translated "beseech, comfort and exhort" and "paraklesis" means "consolation." The same root word describes the Holy Spirit, so "Encourager" or "Comforter" is a name for the God who "draws alongside"!

Paul was a great encourager and urged others to do the same. In 2 Timothy 4:2 he calls Timothy to "rebuke and *encourage* – with great patience . . ." In Hebrews 3:13 the writer compels us all to "*encourage* one another daily." In Acts 9 Barnabas, whose name literally means "son of *encouragement*," took the recently converted Paul, feared by all, into the church in Jerusalem. Later, from Antioch, he led Paul out in ministry. So Barnabas is a model of encouragement in the New Testament.

Educationalists, business managers and team builders are all discovering the importance of approval and endorsement in creating a strong workforce. In educational research it was revealed that, to successfully bring one act of correction into a child's life, the child needed to have been encouraged on seven previous occasions. These days disapproval and judgement seem to be a means of discipline, how can we expect to produce confidence and hope in our communities? Christians must take a lead in reversing this situation and fathering is vital in the process.

Discipline

Discipline is an essential part of growing up and training, but it must be exercised in a context of approval. Hebrews 12:1–12 clearly sets out the argument for discipline. It identifies discipline with love, and cites love as the motivation. The passage draws heavily on the father/son relationship, making it central to the expression of care. We cannot truly love someone and leave them in darkness, ignorance or immaturity. Love compels us to reach out, and that will involve discipline; there's no other way.

Every scholar knows learning demands discipline, just as athletes know that success requires total commitment. To endure hardship we need a goal – wealth, glory, fame or even personal satisfaction. For some the challenge itself is the all-consuming passion, but the greatest motivator is love. Love is a powerful inspiration to achievement and should be the bedrock on which discipline is built. First experiences of discipline should come from a parent who longs for his child to succeed, then trust comes even when pain is involved. So, "make love your aim."

A father's discipline is not detached as that of a coach or tutor, and example plays a great part. Fathers do not simply demand, "Do as I say," but "Do as I do." They model what they teach. Paul in 1 Corinthians 4:14–16 says, "I am not writing this to shame you, but to warn you, as my dear children. Even though you have ten thousand guardians in Christ, you do not have many fathers, for in Christ Jesus I became your father through the gospel. Therefore I urge you to *imitate me*" (my italics.) Discipline and discipleship are largely missing from our church programmes and relationships. The price we pay is seen in our lackadaisical approach to the Christian life.

Release

Discipline has an end in view; it encourages the child to grow up, mature and take their place in life. Thwaites, in *The Church Beyond the Congregation*, underlines this:

> The Garden is not the creation, the nest is not the sky, the nursery is not the city, the mother's milk is not the only thing on the menu of life. Everywhere we look we see the progression from initial safety and simple definition into a more complex and far-reaching world where maturity waits for us alongside our inheritance.

A good father does not breed dependence but prepares for release. The stages of discipleship Jesus used were fourfold – i) watch me while I do it, ii) do it with me, iii) I'll watch you while you do it, and iv) you go and do it on your own. Jesus invested all he was into his disciples, then released them and took pride in their success, encouraging them to "greater works." He was not threatened by them appearing to achieve more, but excited by the prospect.

Jesus' disciples had no contract to ensure they wouldn't start a church nearby; indeed, planting churches was the whole point – the more the merrier! The needs were so great, the management of the few sheep already in the fold was not the focus. It was the millions waiting to hear the good news that spurred them on. Jesus was not a control freak finding fulfillment in being needed or a masochist in the pain of the task. His joys were pleasing the Father, empowering friends and saving the lost.

Jesus passed on authority with responsibility in his final instructions, "All authority in heaven and on earth has been given to me. Therefore go and make disciples of all nations,"

(Matthew 28:18–19). His earthly work completed for the time being, he commissioned and released his team. Similarly, Paul empowered and sent his spiritual daughters and sons, "I commend to you our sister Phoebe . . . give her *any* help she may need from you . . ." (Romans 16:1–2), "I am sending to you Timothy, my son . . . he will remind you of my way . . ." (1 Corinthians 4:17). Are we, as fathers, investing in a new generation who will faithfully nurture and carry forward the work we've begun?

Whilst ministering in Brazil with my colleague Ian Farr we spent three days visiting one of the largest churches in that country, Lagoinha Baptist Church in Belo Horizonte. They were 20,000 strong at the time of writing and expected to double their numbers by the end of 2002. The pastor, Mario Valadão, a fatherly man and extremely humble took us out for a meal. He was keen to learn from our experiences but we were there to draw from him.

We had already discovered that he ran the church, with its 500 full-time workers and 100 ministries, on trust and faith – regularly praying in finance at the end of each month. We asked him the secret of his success. "No secret," he said, "if someone committed to the church has a vision or wants to fulfil their calling, I simply ask two questions – what do you want to do? and, what do you need to do it? Then it's all systems go and people are allowed to make mistakes." We were duly impressed.

Wisdom

For the first five years of a child's life Daddy knows everything. At school it's teacher who knows everything. In their teens they know everything. In their twenties they're amazed to find out how much Dad has learned since they were kids! Wisdom is needed in the early stages of a child's upbringing, but every father in touch with God will have a deep well of experience from which his children can draw long after they're grown up and released from parental authority.

The child becomes the adult, the apprentice the practitioner, the disciple the teacher, and the fatherly role changes from authority to counsel, to advice. The responsibility moves from the father to teach the child, to the adult to draw on from the father. This also applies in the spiritual realm. In John's first letter he says, "I write to you, fathers, because you have known him who is from the beginning" (1 John 2:13); he differentiates between fathers, young people, and children. Those who have a history in Christ should have a deep reservoir of wisdom.

The book of Proverbs was written by a father who wanted to ensure that his son had access to everything his parents had learned. Chapter 1:8 says, "Listen, my son, to your father's instruction and do not forsake your mother's teaching. They will be a garland to grace your head and a chain to adorn your neck." Solomon had made it clear in verse 7: "The fear of the Lord is the beginning of knowledge, but fools despise wisdom and discipline." I wonder how long Jesus spent imbibing the truth in those sayings? Even as a boy his wisdom confounded the rabbis and throughout his ministry he demonstrated wisdom which surpassed that of Solomon.

Parenthood

Before moving on let me return to comment further on a couple of issues. Firstly, that of gender and parenthood. I mentioned the difficulty I had to overcome to speak about "fathers" and not "parents." In part this is because neither fatherhood nor motherhood can be limited to gender. No one is so completely male or female that they display none of the other's attributes. Many men have strong maternal instincts and vice versa. I'm not talking here of sexuality or role reversal; that is an entirely different matter. God is neither male nor female; he is Spirit, nevertheless he displays the attributes of masculinity and femininity. When making man in his own image he put all his traits into us; we're just like him!

In Isaiah 66:12–13 the Lord describes himself in feminine terms, "As a mother comforts her child, so will I comfort you." In Hebrews 5:11–14 the feminine and masculine aspects of a teacher are represented as one who first feeds with milk, feminine, and later with meat, masculine. Elsewhere Paul refers to himself as a nursing mother (1 Thessalonians 2:7).

The name "El Shaddai," "all sufficient one," can be rendered "breasted one," reflected in the Revelation 1 description of Jesus. From a creational view, God did not make man so completely male that he had no need of breasts, or to put it bluntly – nipples. These have no other function than to remind us of our deep and eternal connection to women. Jesus himself carried that reminder in his body too. Only as man and woman together do we fully represent the God in whose image we were made.

Discipleship

Secondly, I must revisit the matter of discipleship. Making disciples not getting decisions, is the way Jesus commissioned us to engage the nations. Discipleship seems longwinded and laborious, and mass decisions appear to be a speedier way of extending the kingdom. A decision is a first step but we all know the appalling statistics of fall-out if there is no commitment to discipleship.

Dallas Willard, addressing discipleship as the missing factor in today's church, says in *The Divine Conspiracy*:

... it is not the much discussed moral failures, financial abuses or the amazing similarity between Christians and non-Christians. These are only effects of the underlying problem. The fundamental negative reality among Christians believers now is their failure to be constantly learning how to live their lives in "the kingdom among us".

The sad truth about many Christians is that the only thing that marks us out from the rest of the population is a decision to accept Christ. Our basic behaviour is the same as everyone else's. We urgently need clarity on this whole area of schooling in life, to which Jesus dedicated his time with that motley crew he gathered around him. Just look at the results! Here are some questions we should consider as leaders:

What does it mean to be a disciple of Jesus?

Must we decide to become a disciple of Jesus? Can we drift into discipleship?

Is it important that both disciple and discipler choose to be involved in the relationship?

What is the cost of discipleship and how can we joyfully embrace the sacrifices?

What part do daily work and family relationships play in discipleship?

Is it important to identify teachers who can challenge us and input our lives?

How can we maintain an attitude of voluntary response rather than automatic submission?

How does our cultural conditioning affect our response to discipleship?

Jesus' command to make disciples of all nations was given to apostles. The concept of God's call being passed on to the whole body is obvious in the Old and New Testaments. Romans 12:1 calls us to offer ourselves as living sacrifices to discover what God's good, pleasing and perfect will is. This is not a divine mystery the Lord is reluctant to make known to us. Exactly the reverse! God longs to share his heart with those who are itching to do his will and fathers are a vital part of restructuring the church for life and growth.

PART III

The church in change

CHAPTER 13

THE MOBILE CHURCH – MOBILIZED!

The church comes out

Earthquakes get people on to the streets! Streaming columns of people carrying precious bundles of possessions, pushing the injured on carts, shoving, dragging unwilling animals and frightened children to safety are not an uncommon sight in the aftermath of disaster.

The angels encouraged Lot's family to flee the city before its destruction. Now the Spirit comes to warn the church of the coming collapse of the world system, already visible in the failure of formal religion. At the same time within every tradition the true church is being revealed. She has started the journey from the place of her exile to the promised land. The divisions in Christendom are not now so much vertical between denominations, as horizontal between those hungry for God and those committed to the structures.

We hear the call, ". . . what fellowship can light have with darkness? . . . What agreement is there between the temple of God and idols? . . . 'Therefore come out from them and be separate,' says the Lord" (2 Corinthians 6:14–18). We've seen the

Greek for church, "ekklesia," has in its meaning the concepts of "called out," and "gathered with a purpose." God's people are called to be moving with a mission. The idea of the church as an apostolic company has mobility at the heart. It's impossible to be a "sent" or a "going" people without movement.

Out of what?

To "come out" or "be separate" is not encouraging separatism or spiritual arrogance. There's a special breed of Christian who feel they alone have the mind of Christ. Quite the opposite, we must repent and forsake such an unholy attitude. The wisdom of God is in the body of Christ and the humble will seek it out through honest, loving relationships. Being separate does not mean leaving our denominations or networks. That's only necessary when they become an obstacle to obedience, when traditions or teachings contradict scripture, as with the Pharisees in Jesus' day.

No, being separate means forsaking ignorance, wrong attitudes, complacency, passivity and worldliness. These things invade our thinking and practices and destroy faith. We wake up to find we are governed by the need for financial security, the demands of a middle-class way of life or carnal diaconates and committees. Surely, the fear of man is one of the most crippling hindrances to a progressive relationship with Father. Let's cast aside these life-sapping bondages and return to the way of faith, the way which our forefathers knew well.

Mobile from the very start

An oasis is welcome in a desert, but rivers have cities built on their banks. Mobility is necessary for growth and development. From earliest times God's people were mobile. Abraham and

Sarah were called out from security and riches to journey to the unknown. Before Abraham, Noah and his family made their incredible passage into a new world. Through opposition and many trials, Moses led Israel out of bondage, to the land God had given them. Even when the people settled, their enemies subdued, there was movement as tribes gathered to fast, pray, and celebrate together.

Imagine the anticipation in the eyes of children as parents, aunts and uncles, and grandparents made ready to go up to Jerusalem for the feast of tabernacles. The harvest safely gathered in, it was time to give thanks, to express their unity as a nation; to celebrate God's promise of Messiah with the blessings of an age to come. Remote villagers would begin their journey first. Gathering belongings on to donkey or cart, they would set out days before the great feast, calling to friends and neighbours to hurry and join them on the way. Numbers grew from village to village, chattering and singing as they went, until the roads were a mass of jostling humanity.

Nearing the city, excitement increased, the streets alive with musicians, dancers and the cries of salesmen plying their wares, each one vying for attention. The air was full of strange smells and sounds invading the senses and demanding a response. A hint of precious perfume gave way to the mouth-watering aroma of baking bread. The cooing of doves carefully carried in a wooden cage, lovingly reared as a sacrifice by some poor family. Sheep, goats, oxen and mules, all are strangely at home in the bustling street traffic. The shouts of recognition, the hugs, the tears of joy and the questions, questions as friends from afar meet.

Multiplication

From north, south, east and west they came – God's people, to worship in his temple. Twelve tribes uniting in a common desire to honour the one true God, Jehovah, their provider and deliverer, giving thanks for his goodness, seeking his mercy and praying for protection. One people, one nation, one Lord, one life; there's no dualism here. Heaven and earth meet in every transaction, emotion, conversation, and song. When this people are at peace with their God, he dwells among them. The nations watch in wonder as they follow this divine romance, a glimpse of God's future for all!

At Pentecost, after the resurrection of Jesus, the Father's inclusive heart bubbled over, pouring out this love on all peoples. Suddenly the circle of acceptance into God's family was enlarged. Now there is room for every people named on earth. The promise to Abraham is fulfilled. We all have an invitation to participate in the heavenly love affair, the marriage – Christ and his church.

If the Gentile church is to provoke Israel as Paul says, winning them back to fellowship with God accepting Yeshua as Messiah, we must be seen to be enjoying the benefits of the kingdom which is rightfully theirs. Jewish people will not be impressed with a lifestyle less attractive than that which they esteem blessed. The kingdom of heaven among us must break down every barrier to unity with Jesus and one another. Poverty and injustice will be banished. Peoples from all cultures will be received and affirmed. The supernatural power of the Holy Spirit will be manifestly with us. The boxes which compartmentalize our lives and are foreign to God will be gone and we will take the church to the people, rather than press the people to come to church.

One people with one purpose

For most Christians the idea of mission is a low-agenda item. That's why missionary societies exist as separate organizations to counter the lack of interest in reaching the lost. The church failed to facilitate the growing numbers who wanted to serve the Lord as evangelists or missionaries. They were not encouraged, properly supported or given frameworks for accountability. This situation remains to this day.

This lack of involvement gives rise to all kinds of problems, including missionary break-down and fall-out, rogue missionaries and parochial local churches. In addition, much of our evangelism has been motivated by pressure, guilt and condemnation. These attitudes come from ignorance and failure to understand the true nature of church and our heavenly commission.

We are one people, one nation under God; as such we are called to be salt and light together. Unless we recognize this, mission will always be an added extra rather than our central focus. If we allow the Spirit to unite us in life and purpose under Jesus our head, missionary activity will explode as city church and mobile church bring skills and resources together. It will not be, "You are lost and need to be saved" but "Come travel with us, be saved with us." The excitement of the journey, with the divine presence and signs of the kingdom among us, will compel others to join our ranks.

Our message today is geared to answer questions no one is asking, rather than provoking enquiry by who we are and what's taking place. Not so in the early church. Just look at the questions: "Brothers, what should we do?" "What must I do to be saved?" "Look, here is water, why shouldn't I be baptized?" Instead, our fruitless, barren and powerless lives and often boring meetings are more a turn-off than a provocation to get involved.

Not that we're totally uncaring, but our longings for God are buried under the demands of life and the responsibilities of running the church. We have lost contact with reality and how the world views us; kingdom values have been exchanged for the values of the age we live in. We have little original to offer the hungry soul but more of the same with an overlay of religion.

Effective witnesses

The word "witness" is one we shy away from. It has connotations of embarrassing door knocking, aggressive preaching or grabbing people to ask if they've been "washed in the blood." Witnessing has become an obligation; we do it reluctantly, with no sense of fulfillment, or not at all and feel guilty. Acts 1:8 does not say, "you *must* be a witness" but "you *will* be my witnesses" (my italics.) It is a promise with no hint of condemnation. It was given to an expectant people, not to a pressurized individual. It's good news and is so precious that we would die for the right to share it and to keep the truth alive. That's why the Greek word "witness" came to mean "martyr."

Five qualities are necessary if our communities are to be effective witnesses for Jesus. First, our corporate witness must be rooted in the tangible presence and power of the Holy Spirit in every believer, especially when we come together. Second, our testimony and message must be in tune. Who we are must coincide with what we say. Third, changed lives and restored relationships must validate our story. Fourth, miracles must be in view confirming God's word. Fifth, we must be willing to suffer, for if our story is not worth dying for can it really be true?

All these factors were present in the early church and are the reasons for their success, in spite of other weaknesses. So, we are witnesses to Christ's kingdom and also herald the demise of Satan's rule – he is not a happy devil!

Accessible and visible church

In our instant society we expect immediate results from investments or we give up. The church must rediscover faith and the ability to persist. The first Christians were so affected by the events surrounding Jesus' death and resurrection they trusted his promises and waited for answers to prayer. They believed God; the rest followed.

Let's learn from their experiences and break out of our narrow mindsets. Let's embrace a biblical understanding of church, as the active, dynamic presence of God among us influencing every aspect of life, work and worship: ordinary people walking and working with an extraordinary God. The church will be accessible, the shallow edges out in society and the deeps more visible and attractive to those who long for meaning to life. The pure river flowing from God's throne will provide a desirable alternative to the flood of filth, lies and violence pouring from the dragon's mouth (Revelation 12:15) which threatens to engulf the world.

24-hour church

One of the great problems in the church today is the limitations of our gatherings, especially for those who meet only once or twice a week.

Thwaites comments in *Church Beyond the Congregation*: "Marriage, family and work fill the creation; meetings, programmes and building cannot. When the local gathering attempts to encompass the impossible it cannot help but falter" and in *The McDonaldization of the Church*, Drane, speaking of reaching the hedonists in our ranks, says:

> . . . an effective spirituality for those attracted to the hedonistic lifestyle will need to be an embodied spirituality, which can understand play as worship, and see God's kingdom as a party (both very scriptural notions). Almost by definition, therefore, they will probably not be reached by a church which meets in the traditional way on

Sunday mornings. Indeed, in the first instance they will probably not be reached by a church which meets during the day at all.

Today we are completely unable to serve the needs of our people, even when they come from a single class or group. Worship styles, music, methods of imparting truth, integrating the generations are just some of the difficulties.

Those who work with young people have enormous struggles trying to settle them in even the liveliest of churches. Youth, or specialized churches may help but are not the full answer, since no single church can supply the breadth and diversity required. These problems are multiplied when we have growth as people have high expectation of the meeting and a low commitment to church. We must reverse this.

24-hour church is the answer! Not a mega-store obliterating competition but a co-operative of large and local corner shops, working together to provide every part of the community with what is needed for life and living. Impossible, you say! Not at all. If we maintain our diversity and combine our resources it can be done. Then, any time of the day or night, those in need would know exactly where to go to find help and hope. In this "mix and match" world we must upgrade to serve the complex community in which we live, providing our kingdom values are maintained.

We already have 24-hour prayer, (I refer to "24–7" elsewhere). American teacher and author, Mike Bickle, is developing 24-hour, 7 days a week worship in his "House of Prayer" ministry in Kansas City. It's time for 24-hour, 7 days a week church where busy business people, single mums, the homeless, the elderly and artists alike can all find a welcome and a place to be at home. Only co-operation can deliver such a vision but the breakthrough will come.

CHAPTER 14

THE PRIMARY PURPOSE AND ESSENTIAL INGREDIENTS OF CHURCH

Rediscovering our radical roots

John Major called the British "back to basics", a call that applies in many other parts of the world too. Years ago, in reaction to Victorian legalism and restraint we threw off the shackles and ran to free expression. Humanism said that in the right environment, our basic goodness would rise to the surface. So away with unhealthy restrictions and inhibitions. No area was sacrosanct, be it business, politics, education, health, the arts or even family life.

Decades on we have paid the price. Children who cannot read, write or count; politicians with no moral code; business people whose word counts for nothing; nurses and teachers not valued and with no sense of vocation, and the breakdown of family with all its terrible consequences. These are some of the costs, and the church is no exception to this collapse and loss of moral bearings.

Going back to the past, or to "Egypt" as the Bible puts it, is not the answer. The history of church and society is full of staggerings from left to right, from crippling law to sentimental grace, from one political or religious extreme to another, in our efforts to find reality and purpose apart from God. No, we must rediscover God's heart and establish his absolutes of truth in our lives again.

Jesus said, "I will build my church" and against his church the gates of hell will not prevail. It is not just a question of changing the structures or becoming more relevant, it is much more fundamental. The supernatural life of God and his values of mercy and judgement must permeate everything.

We have become preoccupied with buildings, finance, meetings and the way we do things, whereas Chinese Christians as revival spreads are more concerned with relationships, spontaneity and holiness. As children we are taught that church is a building with a steeple or a cross on it, and has little to do with life and living. At best we see it as a point of reference in times of great life events such as births, weddings and funerals. At worst it is an object of ridicule and hatred.

Worship – a relationship with God

Like many today the woman Jesus met at the well had given up on religion. She saw the hypocrisy and sought life elsewhere. She was unimpressed by worship the Samaritan way, on the mountain, or the Jewish way, in the temple: neither had meaning for her. Jesus cut through it all and said, in effect, what many say who have nothing to do with Christianity, "You don't have to go to church to be a Christian. It's what you believe and how you behave that counts." Of course, people who say that neither go to church nor behave properly: it's an excuse. Nevertheless, *where* we worship God is of little consequence and *how* we worship is of the utmost importance.

Worship is the outcome of a relationship with God, and our primary reason for existence. It is our duty and delight and must be done in Spirit and in truth. It's to do with heart and will, with emotion and obedience. It is individual and corporate, and we need both. Jesus died to reinstate a worshipful relationship between men and God. He reconnected the body to the head and brought harmony between earth and heaven.

Quality and quantity

God is Spirit and all the analogies to the Holy Spirit in scripture are flexible and fluid. Wind, fire, breath, oil and water help us identify some aspect of his nature. So, above all, the church alive in the Spirit, must express that fluidity and flexibility by displaying the characteristics of the God who is Spirit and truth.

Once we are behaving properly as church, like God, we will be able to fill any space or shape anywhere in the world with life. Buildings and structures will be relatively unimportant except to serve life. Through his people, the glory of God will fill the earth as waters cover the sea. Our chief concern will be for the quality of life filling the space, rather than the shape of the space, for what is contained in the vessel rather than the vessel.

There is an amazing story of a widow's rewarded faith in 2 Kings 4. The woman, wife of a dead prophet, was left with two sons and her husband's debt – what kind of inheritance are *we* passing on? Creditors were about to take her sons as slaves and all she possessed was "a little oil." A telling picture of the Western church, spiritually destitute, about to be taken into slavery but, like the widow, we have a "little oil." We are not completely without the Holy Spirit. The woman cried to Elisha, who commanded her to collect all the empty vessels she could, beg or borrow. "Don't just ask for a few!" he warned.

Every available space

She visited neighbours gathering jars, jugs and pots of every shape and size. Then the prophet called her and her sons to pour out the oil. Wonder of wonders, the tiny bottle did not stop until every vessel was full, sufficient to pay every debt and enough for the family for the rest of their lives. Oh, the miracle of God's provision! Jesus, our Elisha, has the answer, and the oil of the Spirit will fill every vessel we present to him.

Let's pour into the pots of lives gathered in homes and cells, office prayer groups, schools, colleges, hospitals, workplaces, pubs. Wherever there are a few empty pots gathered the oil will continue to flow. "I will pour out my Spirit on all people," the Lord promised Joel 2:28. Peter claimed that promise and passed it on to those responding and to all who long for God's blessing in their lives today (Acts 2:17 & 38–39).

Wineskins and wine

Structure is necessary, but it is the life of God at work within which makes the difference. Oil with no pots would be wasted, poured on the ground, as has happened in many a revival. A river without banks is an uncontrollable flood and a body without bones a quivering jelly. Nevertheless, banks do not make a river, nor do bones, however beautifully arranged, make a living body.

Scripture also speaks of wine, wineskins and the quality of the wine. Without a skin or a bottle there is no way of containing the wine, but I have seldom heard anyone admiringly say, "Wow, what a great bottle! What a wonderful wineskin!" If that happens it means the producer is marketing an inferior product. Necessary though they are, wineskins and bottles are a means to an end. The end is the wine and the flavour of the vintage.

In the 1960s I learned the importance of wineskins when we experienced revival in a local school. Two teachers had been praying for an outpouring of the Holy Spirit. For some years a non-charismatic Christian teacher had provided a consistent work which gave boys regular teaching and opportunities to meet during term time and through the long holidays. He worked hard; there was not much wine but there was a suitable wineskin. A steady stream of lads came to Christ and were processed into church, some carrying on into ministry and missionary service.

My two friends were Spirit-filled, and through them the Lord moved in remarkable ways. In one term more than 200 boys responded to the gospel. Boys wept walking from one lesson to another under conviction of the Spirit. The headmaster, not a Christian, saw this and asked the boys why they were crying. "It's sin sir, we need forgiveness" was the reply. Some lads were thrown across the classroom, delivered from demons; others were healed. The school bubbled with life. Each morning a group gathered for prayer before school and the supernatural was commonplace.

When the summer came there was no provision for fellowship during the holidays. There was no wineskin in place. For young immature Christians this was a disaster. When they returned the next term all but two had backslidden. Those two remain to this day, but had we provided for the boys through the break those statistics could have been very different. The life of God was there, but there was no structure to preserve it. In the first church the rich harvest of wine was contained in a wineskin carefully prepared by Jesus.

Jerusalem experiment or prototype

From its inception the early church enjoyed the benefits of heavenly wine and oil. Reconciliation, uninhibited joy, newfound boldness, enthusiasm and supernatural gifts were some of the blessings its members experienced in the wake of the Holy Spirit's arrival. There was also leadership and a network of relationships left in place by Jesus. The new church enjoyed new life, but was able to facilitate growth and development through apostolic care.

Theologians have called what was described in Acts chapters 2 to 4 as the "Jerusalem Experiment" – an optimistic attempt to build the ideal church which could never last. Breakdown and division, they say, were inevitable and the system of denominations we have must suffice until the Lord comes. Rubbish! The same Holy Spirit who worked in the barren religious community of Judaism 2,000 years ago to give birth to the radical infant church, can do it again for the wayward Gentile church of today.

If we allow him, the Spirit will rearrange our behaviour, plant a passion for his will within us and give us love and appreciation for fellow-believers. Generosity and hospitality will abound, as will miracles and healings. There will be a fresh devotion to apostolic teaching, prayer and fellowship as we see ourselves as God's alternative community of faith. We'll be a bridgehead to establish tomorrow's kingdom, under Satan's nose, today – a sign that Jesus' victory is effective in our generation. Now, if the primary purpose of the church is to worship God in Spirit and truth, to provide a home through which the Holy Spirit can make Jesus known, what will be the main ingredients of this church?

Discovering church . . .

As a teenager, disillusioned and unimpressed with Christianity, I went to discover what the world had to offer. Carnal pleasures and fascination with the occult soon had me in their grip, but the reality of evil I encountered led me back to search for God. The simplicity and power Christine and I found in the church of Acts grabbed our attention. We experienced a remarkable deliverance and baptism in the Holy Spirit, and began our quest to see a more biblical church established as a working model. We wanted to encourage other Christians to believe that New Testament Christianity was for our generation too.

In East London with a handful of newly converted young people we sought to embody the uncomplicated lifestyle, passionate worship and missionary zeal of the Acts. We moved to be near one another and opened our homes. We shared our money and possessions so there was little need among us. Creativity was released in worship and there was a high expectancy that the Holy Spirit would work in our lives.

If the Acts of the Apostles taught us how the church should behave in public, we soon learned that the Epistles were given so that we would know how to behave in private. The natural progression was into the book of Revelation to see how the church would fare in the future. Life was exciting and the likelihood of Jesus returning in our generation seemed a real possibility.

Things were good, very good. However, as I've said, with the passage of time we began to preach the gospel of the church and community life, rather than the gospel of Jesus. We missed the fact that before Acts, the Epistles and Revelation, came those four important and often overlooked books, the Gospels. The painful lessons we learned prepared us for the next stage of our journey.

. . . Jesus style

It is obvious to me now that the Gospels tell us what Jesus had to say about church and are the foundation upon which all else is built. Jesus' ministry was full of teaching on how we should live as his people and we must seek to apply all we see in the Gospels, but in Matthew chapters 16 and 18 we find the essential ingredients of church.

In these passages the master reveals the absolute basics without which church cannot exist. First, and most importantly, he speaks of our relationship to him and second, he speaks of our relationship to one another. These ingredients are inextricably linked together. Like sand and cement they provide a base on which we can build that which cannot be shaken. In the next chapter we'll explore these key scriptures.

CHAPTER 15

TWO BASIC INGREDIENTS

1 – A relationship with Jesus (Matthew 16:13–19)

Jesus the source!

Jesus refers to church directly on only two occasions. This first time, in Matthew 16, he journeyed with his disciples to Caesarea Philippi, one of the northernmost places of his ministry. It seems it was necessary for him to visit this particular town and what happened here was a watershed in the lives and understanding of the apostles.

Caesarea Philippi was the source of the Jordan, for here its waters gushed from a rock. In view of the remarkable symbolism, it is likely this was the spot where Jesus took his disciples to question them about his origins. On one side of the rock was carved an effigy of Caesar, the man who claimed he was God. On the other side was Pan, the god who tried to become man. Both failed miserably. Now the One who was fully Son of Man and Son of God stood before them. The Rock of God where divinity and humanity met in perfect harmony and from which the healing waters of life flowed. As yet, Jesus' followers had not guessed who he really was but speculation abounded.

"Who do people say the Son of Man is?" the Lord asked. Their replies confirmed the confusion among those who heard his teaching and saw the miracles. John the Baptist, Elijah, Jeremiah or one of the prophets had all been overheard. "But what about you?" Jesus asked. "Who do you say I am?" We need to use our imagination to grasp what was happening. Like the rest, Peter was frantically searching the corners of his brain for inspiration. Suddenly the unthinkable blasted its way to the front of his mind. "You are the Christ" he whispered, hardly daring to let the words past his lips, "You are the Son of the living God!"

Peter – a rock?

With sharp intakes of breath the others waited on tenterhooks to see what their master's reaction would be. What they heard seemed to be blasphemy of the highest order. To their amazement he did not rebuke impetuous Peter, but confirmed his words. "Blessed are you Simon (meaning 'hearing') son of Jonah, for this was not revealed to you by man, but by my Father in heaven." As if this was not enough he went on, "And I tell you that you are Peter [meaning 'little rock' or 'stone'] and on this rock I will build my church, and the gates of Hades will not overcome it." Thus Jesus set theologians arguing for centuries.

Was Peter, a mere man, the rock on which Jesus would build his church, or was he himself the foundation of the new Jerusalem? Catholics and Protestants still debate the question, but the answer is not in the extremes. In this, as in most doctrinal matters, the Bible is its own interpreter. It is clear from such scriptures as 1 Corinthians 3:11, Ephesians 2:20 and Revelation 21:14, Jesus is the foundation on which *we* build, but apostles and prophets are the foundation on which *he* builds. Ministry builds on Jesus, and Jesus builds on his chosen ministries. But, remember, important though foundations are, they are not the building – the building is the building.

Living stones

So, if Jesus is "the rock," and apostles and prophets are "little rocks," then the people are living stones which make the building. The focus of Jesus and his servant ministries is always people. Together, we are being built into a temple not made with human hands but by the Spirit as a dwelling place for God. Now, what makes a stone suitable for inclusion in this building?

This too is obvious in the context of the scripture we're looking at. It is the revelation and confession of who Jesus is which separates granite from crumbly man-made bricks. Religious bricks may look good but they will not last. Endurance is a necessary feature of all materials used in this construction. So we see the primary ingredient of church is a present, active revelation and confession of who God's Son really is. Put simply, it is a living relationship with Jesus Christ which guarantees us a permanent place in the kingdom.

Yielding gates

The results of receiving and speaking out this truth are so profound, no power in heaven or on earth can resist it. Even Hades' gates must yield. There was a time when I pictured the gates of death and hell moving against the church to swallow her up. The church just hung on until Jesus returned. Then, one day, the Lord whispered, "Son, gates don't move!" "Whoops!" I revised my picture, putting God's people on the offensive, fearlessly attacking the gates to release those held captive by sickness, sin and death. This was another step but still far from God's intention.

In the first scenario the church is passive, in the second she is active in her own strength, but Jesus' way is trust and faith – "I will give you the keys!" Gates were made to be unlocked. Jesus has the keys of the kingdom and places them into the hands of faithful servants with power to bind or loose. No hanging on, no striving, just walking in the victory Jesus has secured for us. A church shaken and stirred will shake and stir the society in which she exists.

All authority

The promise Jesus gave to his disciples here, "whatever you bind on earth will be bound in heaven, and whatever you loose on earth will loosed in heaven," is repeated in Matthew 18[1]. Then, in Matthew 28:18–19, he commissions them with assurance, "All authority in heaven and on earth has been given to me. Therefore (you) go (with this same authority) and make disciples of all nations" (brackets mine).

Those who have a revelation of who Jesus is, and are willing to confess it, even at cost to themselves, are candidates for authority to be entrusted to them. They have taken the first and most important step into the power zone. This power is ours, not as a result of physical, material or military might, but by embracing the cross. The second step, which establishes God's authority in our lives, is our relationship with fellow believers. We will explore this second ingredient shortly.

Small beginnings but certain end

Before we leave Matthew 16, let's look at one more thing. Up to this point, no one had grasped the incredible truth of who Jesus was. Now, one man on earth, a simple fisherman, had seen the light but was unaware of the consequences. Such was Jesus' confidence in the Holy Spirit's ability to spread the truth he could move on to Jerusalem to suffer and die. What Peter had seen could not be unseen. This mighty truth would spread like a virus of blessing wherever there were receptive hearts. The future was secure, and nothing could stop this life-giving truth. The evidence is here as 2,000 years on it has reached us today and will continue its work until the kingdom of heaven is established in every tribe and nation.

2 – Relationships with one another (Matthew 18:15–20)

From vertical to horizontal relationships

In Matthew 18:15 Jesus moves from the *vertical*, our relationship to God, to the *horizontal*, our relationship to one another. The cross is a wonderful symbol of this. In his death Jesus reconciled us with our Father in heaven and stretched out his hands to reconcile us to each other. Without the first, the vertical relationship to God, there can be no horizontal relationship with one another. The second, the horizontal member of the cross, hangs on the first, the vertical. We have no hope of lasting relationships in our families, friendships or communities unless they hang on the love and discipline we receive from the Lord.

So Jesus begins, "If your brother . . ." Here 'brother' is a collective term referring to men and women. In his book, *For Such A Time As This* published by Pioneer Direct on the subject of women in leadership, Martin Scott points out that masculine words in Greek and Hebrew can be inclusive, but feminine words are always female. It is important to keep this in mind in a church that has been male-dominated for centuries, where the scriptures have been wrongly interpreted in favour of men, as they once were in favour of slavery!

Reconciliation – a simple process

In this passage Jesus addresses the issues of right attitudes and church discipline. His dealings with us are always remedial, so we too must always strive for restoration, never revenge or self-justification. Where someone is sinned against or there are differences or communication problems, our first concern should be to *"hear"*, to listen closely to what the other has to say.

Most are more anxious to be heard than to understand the other's pain. So frustration comes, bringing hurtful reactions. Confusion and misunderstandings are the inevitable result. Our first aim is not to find agreement, but to *hear* one another. Listening carefully, with a desire to understand, indicates our attitudes are good and we will consider problems honestly. We should also agree to accept judgement and discipline from trusted friends after both perspectives are properly aired.

Sadly few churches take Jesus' instructions seriously, amazing for "Bible believing" Christians! In addition, we talk to everyone else about our problems before the person who offended us, our excuse being we don't want to hurt *them*, which really means *we* don't want to be hurt. Those who do venture to share in this way frequently give up if they fail to make progress. With no pastoral support, this leaves a festering wound. Leadership which does not help follow through the process will see breakdown of the church or a superficial level of relationships.

No wonder people traipse from one church to another and learn to maintain relationships at a distance to avoid pain. For everyone's benefit, we should initiate this straightforward means of reconciliation Jesus gave us. First, share on a one to one basis; second, share together with trusted friends and finally, if the issue persists, "Tell it to the church," all this in the context of watchful and caring leaders.

Which church?

The question arises, what did Jesus mean, "Tell it to the church?" Here, "church" was his apostolic team; at that time there was no other church. Therefore we can assume "church" is that part of the body most relevant to the parties involved, together with appropriate leadership.

Clearly in a local church of hundreds or a city church of thousands, it would be inappropriate to involve everyone in a minor fall-out between two individuals. In this case the smaller relational setting is relevant. Tragically, many Christians have such shallow relationships that the threat of exclusion from their "church" is of little concern. What's more, they would be welcome elsewhere, no questions asked, in some other "church" so discipline is meaningless to them. If relationships are to count and become a witness this must change.

Obviously, this subject deserves much more coverage than is possible here. However, let me say, if Christians are to have a cutting edge in society and judge righteously in cases of evil practice and injustice, we must faithfully examine ourselves first. Ignoring our own sins, particularly in cases of financial corruption, moral failure among leaders, or authority abuse, is not an option. Where sin affects the whole body or is public knowledge, there must be public confession and rebuke (1 Timothy 5:20). Whilst grace and forgiveness are freely available, we must be seen to deal cleanly with unrighteousness in our midst. If we observe these simple principles of fellowship this will release Jesus' authority to bind and loose[2].

Damp squib . . .

Finally, Matthew 18:19–20: remarkable verses so often quoted without real understanding of their import. The enemy has robbed us of the potential to do him serious damage by blinding us to their meaning. Let's examine the latter statement first, as the former finds its power source here. "For where two or three come together in my name, there I am with them." The word "for" is significant, perhaps we would realise how significant if we use *because*. The reason we have power in prayer is because we are gathered in Jesus' name and because he is with us.

If I ask the question, "Where have you heard this scripture most frequently?" the majority reply "The prayer meeting," the rest, "A gathering where only a few people turn up." On these occasions, we add the phrase, *"Well never mind then,* where two or three are gathered . . ." These four words have become part and parcel of how we view this passage. How clever Satan is! Scripture does not say, *"Well never mind then."* A paraphrase might help – "You have power in prayer *because*, where even only two or three are gathered by me into my name, I am with you," says the Lord!'

. . . or powerful rocket?

What should have been a "light the blue touch paper and watch this rocket go into orbit" statement, has become an excuse for depressed prayer group leaders. Friends, the reason why our prayer gatherings are so poorly attended is the lack of faith and expectancy we inspire and the low level of creativity in these meetings.

They also attract church bores who feel free to preach unwanted sermons or deliver criticisms of the church under some prophetic guise. Why do we allow these people to tell God things he knew before the foundation of the world, to prophesy in a poor copy of 1611 English and show off their Bible knowledge from Genesis to Revelation? Thankfully, there's a fresh hunger for God and we are learning to pray in greater reality and in new, creative ways.

I'll come back to this verse in the next chapter, but now let's return to verse 19: "Again, I tell you that if two of you on earth agree about anything you ask for, it will be done for you by my Father in heaven." "Again" indicates we are about to hear a repetition of what has been said, in popular speak "a double whammy." Jesus is underlining the fact that, if we are in right relationship with him and with one another, we can ask anything, bind anything or loose anything, it will be done.

As with the previous statement, this has also been devalued by the devil and by our lack of faith. Having overcome the disappointment of small numbers, we finally get the prayer meeting under way. We identify the things to pray for and make the false assumption that, if the two or three can "agree" about the issues, God is bound by his word to answer because we are agreed. Wrong! This is not what Jesus said.

How to agree and how to ask

The Greek for "agree" is "sumphoneo" – our English word "symphony." This puts a different light on the meaning. For two or three of us to make a "symphony" with our lives, we must consistently be in harmony playing from the same score. Agreement cannot mean we have reached the same level of understanding in all matters of life and doctrine. As we've seen, achieving "unity in the faith" (Ephesians 4:13) is an ongoing process. Right attitudes, mutual submission and a teachable spirit are the qualities needed to be agreeable even in disagreement. We all have tensions but it is how we handle them that matters.

In open, honest and forgiving circles of friendship and commitment the Lord will pour out his grace and hear our prayers. The idea that God will answer simply because we agree about the things we are praying for, when we are out of fellowship or critical and unforgiving, is ludicrous. Here's another paraphrase to help you appreciate what Jesus is saying. "Listen, have you really understood what I was saying about binding and loosing? I'm telling you that if *only two* of you, who are reconciled and in agreement with me, can also make a symphony of agreement in your lives together, you can ask my Father for anything and he will do it!"

Relationships, relationships, relationships

Unity with the Father through Jesus creates the devil-shattering possibility of unity with one another. This puts power in the hands of the weakest saint to deal serious blows to the enemy and sets captives free! These simple ingredients are the basic minimum we need to have visible church. Elders, apostles, buildings, guitars, PA systems, Bible schools, money and the like may be extremely helpful, but the way we live and interact with Jesus as friends and fellow travellers is of paramount importance. There's no church without relationships, the vertical and horizontal members of the cross must be in place.

One person having a relationship with God does not make a church, any more than one beautiful rock makes a temple. John's first letter warns that if we say we love God and do not show love for one another, we are liars. Strong words, but they're true. Love for one another is dependent on love for God and is the evidence that our love for God is genuine. Love for God produces love for each other and love for each other is the visible sign to the world that Jesus is building his church – "see how these Christians love one another."

To summarize, we have really been talking about three ingredients, not two. The first and primary ingredient is a right relationship to Jesus and, through him, to his Father. The second is a right relationship to one another which releases God's power. The third is a relationship with the enemy which enables us to demonstrate Christ's victory in our lives and to the generation of which we are a part. This trinity of truth must be our bedrock if we're to be the overcoming company, the church which will usher in the new age of Jesus' rule on earth.

Notes

1. See Appendix 1: also pages 36 and 155.
2. See Appendix 1: also pages 36 and 152.

CHAPTER 16

CHURCH WITHOUT WALLS

The shapes of the church to come 1 – classic

Overflowing cups . . .

A church which is shaken and stirred is one ready to be poured out. A fluid, flowing church can be poured into a container of any shape. Thus the shapes of the church to come are as varied as the containers we provide. If we worship a God who pours himself out into our lives, how much more should we be poured out on behalf of others? In the light of David's discovery of God's generosity under the old covenant in Psalm 23, "You anoint my head with oil; my cup overflows," what should we, under the blessing of Jesus' new covenant, expect but overflowing cups?

There is a link between anointing with oil and overflowing cups. The Lord pours the oil of the Holy Spirit into our lives and relationships; we overflow with blessing into the world. On Pentecost morning a container of 120 yielded lives was anointed; the vessel overflowed. The infant church, born in an upper room, was immediately poured out on to the streets. What happened then was not a one-off event, to be viewed with envy until Jesus comes. It was a prototype, a first working model on which a million others would be built.

Peter knew it, ". . . this is what was spoken by the prophet Joel: 'In the last days, God says, I will pour out my Spirit on all people' . . . the promise is for you and your children . . ." (Acts 2:16 and 39). He left us in no doubt that what the Lord had begun would continue until his love had encompassed all peoples, of all races, in all times. The glory of Jesus was shared with his followers. This glory was not an ethereal glow as portrayed by some medieval artist. It was real, down to earth glory his disciples saw, full of the "grace and truth" (John 1:14). The overflowing heart of God fills us to overflowing and floods the earth "as the waters cover the sea!" (Habakkuk 2:14).

. . . of every size and shape

Church is a quality of life. It is God's grace and truth expressed in any configuration of human relationships brought together by Jesus. Now we are free to be creative as the Holy Spirit inspires us within the liberating boundaries of his unity and diversity. The church, being an organism before she is organization, will be extremely difficult to categorize or eradicate. Thus, under threat and persecution she not only survives but grows and flourishes.

If what I am saying about the multiplicity of expressions of church is true, we should find many different models in the scripture. We must discover these in order to meet the needs of this post-modern world. Moynagh in *Changing World, Changing Church* says, "in the emerging 'it-must-fit-me' world, if church remains distant and standardised, unable to fit the people it seeks to reach, it will be ignored."

I promised to return to Matthew 18:20 and this verse is the place to begin to examine, firstly, the five classic shapes of church and later the variety within these. We have identified the basic ingredients of church. What is the numerical minimum? Clearly you cannot have relational church with one individual; the necessary "gathered together" element would be missing.

Minimum requirement

So the smallest component of church or cell, the building block of the body of Christ, is two or three gathered together in Jesus' name. Let's call this *micro-church*. "Gathered together" in the Authorized Version is much stronger than "come together" in the New International Version. The Greek is "sunago", from which synagogue comes. It carries a sense of being drawn together as with the membership of a synagogue, implying more than casual or occasional meetings.

The synagogue was where the community met God with purpose, for worship, prayer, instruction and fellowship. It was where friends and neighbours, who shared daily joys in pains and work-a-day life, came to meet God. In our transient society it is good to know that the Lord Jesus is drawing groups of friends together to reflect something permanent in Christian relationships.

From his wide circle of friends Jesus nurtured the kind of intimate relationships we all need. Many disciples followed him and he chose 72 to send out in pairs to carry the kingdom message. The 12, with him throughout his ministry, spent quality time with him. Within the 12 there was an inner circle of Peter, James and John, and finally, John was "the disciple whom Jesus loved." John understood Jesus' heart because he spent so much time with his ear on Jesus' breast (John 21:20).

Linked to a wider family

Micro-church can meet anywhere, any time. On a train journey to work, on a park bench, around the ironing board, at the gym or on the way home from school. Wherever friends, drawn together by Jesus, share a desire to glorify him, that's church in its simplest form. Whilst a cell has all the characteristics of the body in its DNA, one cell does not make a body. Cells are built together in *mini-church* where twos and threes meet in the slightly wider setting of church in the house.

Acts shows that, from the beginning, the home became a centre for church life and activity. The family was not the modern nuclear family, of mum, dad and two or three children which, even in this limited concept of family, is seriously breaking down today. It was an extended family, with aunts and uncles, grandparents, servants and helpers sharing life and responsibilities. These relational networks meant that whole households, wider families and even an entire village or area, could be influenced by the gospel. Today there are so few networks like these, that soul-winning is extremely hard and usually has to be on a one-to-one basis.

I've avoided identifying micro-church or mini-church as a family unit. This is deliberate, as I do not believe that the family is the building block of the church. Family is the building block of society, and needs to be upheld as such. When families break down society is under threat. God has given us a social order which we must maintain. However, churches built around a family, even husband and wife leadership, create an unnatural environment which may become exclusive.

Families are important but must be inclusive and open to cross-fertilization which is healthy. In this kind of church single people and single-parent families, young and old, are honoured and respected and can play their part from leadership through to all areas of church life. I am not implying that God can never use a family or husband and wife team, but this is the exception. As an itinerant ministry I have seen the sad effects of family-dominated churches at home and abroad, where status or leadership is given on the basis of blood ties rather than calling, gift or ability.

Church in the house

The biblical evidence for church in the house is irrefutable, and it's hard to imagine why denominations, many of which started with cottage meetings, are so threatened by fresh movements in that direction. In Acts they broke bread in their homes (2:46); they taught in the temple and from house to house (5:42); in his attempts to break up the church, Paul went from house to house because that's where they met (8:3); in Ephesus Paul taught publicly and from house to house (20:20). In 1 Timothy Paul warned of busybodies spreading gossip from one home to another (5:13), and in Titus of false teachers who were "ruining whole households" with deception (1:11).

There are also specific references to church in the house. In Romans 16:5 Paul greets the church in the home of Priscilla and Aquila and in 1 Corinthians 16:19 he does the same. In Colossians 4:15 he speaks of Nympha and the church in her house. Interestingly in all three of these references a woman was probably the key leader, having received a primary mention.

None of this takes account of the many passages which indirectly confirm that church exists wherever people meet, in home, temple court, around meal tables or on the streets. Nor does it acknowledge that Jesus clearly instructed his disciples to use homes when travelling in ministry. Wherever they were welcomed, the home became a base for preaching and teaching (Luke 9:4). Why, 2,000 years later, do we feel we know better than Jesus?

By focusing on the home Jesus established a timeless, cross-cultural principle which rooted church firmly in relationships and society. This scuppered ghetto mentality and avoided superficiality in all expressions of church. He also provided the means of fast and unlimited church growth, as Wolfgang Simson points out in *Houses that Change the World*, OM Publishing:

> The fruit of an apple tree is not an apple, but another apple tree. The fruit of a church is not a convert, but other churches that plant other churches.

Diversity and balance

For some Christians their Sunday fix of church can be the least relational thing they do in a non-relational week. This kind of church experience will not draw the masses, many of whom long for companionship in their lonely, monochrome lives. From the grass roots all the way through, church is the vehicle Jesus wants to use to promote kingdom life and give the world a taste of his tomorrow, today.

Within micro-cell church and mini-house church we begin to see the wonderful diversity there is in God's family. Like snow-flakes, no two are alike. Each has its own unique identity and emphasis, be it creativity, hospitality, giving, intercession, prophecy, administration or a thousand other contributions to our lives together.

For this reason we need one another. The limitations of our strengths leave us vulnerable. Balance is not in every individual or small group, but in the body as a whole. When we pronounce a group unbalanced, we usually mean they are different from us. We forget we're unbalanced, as no group or network can be balanced. Balance is in the body, so scripture encourages us "not . . . (to forsake) the assembling of ourselves together" (Hebrews 10:25, AV). The one body, linked in all its parts, ensures the flow of health and understanding until, together, we reach the fullness of Christ.

Assembly points and city churches

Just as micro-church gives way to mini-church, so mini-church must give way to *multi-church* where home churches come together under the care and encouragement of wider leadership. In a large town there may be many local congregations providing home churches with easy access to teaching, discipline, worship, fellowship and communication. This network of relationships spread across an area puts everyone within walking distance of church in one form or another – a little church in every street, each within a car (or donkey) ride of the multi-church assembly. One such local church in Corinth was found in Cenchrea, the eastern harbour area of the city.

Most Protestant Christians see multi-church or local church as the primary expression of church having autonomy and independence. This is unbiblical, as in scripture we see the worldwide church linked through leadership, work, friendship and life, which transcend our unnatural divisions. Our denomination may link us to a national or international network, but even this falls far short of God's best.

As multi-churches flow together *mega-church* or city-wide church emerges. In his letters Paul writes "to the elders of the church in . . ." naming the town or city. Always to one group of elders in one church who were city-wide ministries, not single congregational leaders. A divided church in a town was unthinkable to Paul, as he made clear when he insisted that there be "no divisions among you" (1 Corinthians 1:10).

Visibility

The only occasions where Paul addresses or refers to "churches," plural, are in connection with Galatia or Asia, which are regions. In today's burgeoning cities of millions, where up to 80% of the world's population live, it would not be unreasonable to have a number of mega-churches in different parts of town. However, there must be a high level of co-operation with key leaders meeting for regular times of fellowship and waiting on God for the whole city or conurbation.

If we really believe there is only one church it will be seen in the way we behave. We will serve and encourage others before ourselves and draw from their experience and resources. Competition will be outlawed and edges blurred. Some scholars believe the Ephesian church could have numbered 20,000. Imagine the effect of a crowd this size, united and gathered for worship in some central place, perhaps in front of the temple of Diana – "A city on a hill cannot be hidden" (Matthew 5:14).

Jesus not only calls us to be hidden like salt, with its disinfectant, seasoning and fertilizing properties, scattered through homes, streets and institutions, but also to come together as light. In Jesus' physical absence, empowered by Spirit, we are the light of the world, shining with the character of our coming King and the nature of his kingdom. How different our towns would be if we unitedly expressed our love for God and humanity and our abhorrence for sin and oppression as God intended. The result – the redemption of our communities and ultimately creation itself!

Sharing the blessing and the pain

Even mega-church does not stand alone as church, however successful. Each deposit of church is only a part. This makes sense of Paul's words in 1 Corinthians 12:26, "If one part suffers, every part suffers with it; if one part is honoured, every part rejoices with it." A body truly joined shares the joys and pain of every member.

How could a strong local church ignore the needs of a weaker, struggling one down the road? How could churches in a prosperous nation turn a blind eye to the suffering of churches in oppressed or poor areas of the world? Sadly, this still happens and is evidence that Christ's body is divided. For purely selfish reasons, it makes sense to look after other parts of our own body, but love demands it – "After all, no-one ever hated his own body, but he feeds and cares for it, just as Christ does the church – for we are members of his body" (Ephesians 5:29–30).

The big picture church

Lastly, *macro-church*, or universal church, for which "catholic" is simply another word, is the highest expression of church and most fully represents Jesus. It is the sum-total of God's people in every tribe, people, tongue and nation throughout time – "For we were all baptized by one Spirit into one body" (1 Corinthians 12:13).

Those of previous generations who died before the cross receive their inheritance in Christ by faith. We too receive the gifts of sanctification, unity and maturity by faith and work them out in our lives and relationships on a daily basis. So all God's people, before or after Christ, receive by faith and continue in faith to fullness.

Macro-church, saints past, present and future, is the church for which Jesus is returning. It may only be a remnant who reach fullness and visibly represent the perfect bride prepared for our Lord, but it will be significant. So, we have a vested interest in seeing the church universal come to maturity. Our future, our salvation and the winding up of this age are wrapped up in its success. Charles Wesley knew this as we see from one of his great hymns of eternal length – sorry, eternal *truth*:

> 1. Happy the souls that first believed,
> To Jesus and each other cleaved;
> Joined by the unction from above,
> In mystic fellowship of love.

2. Meek, simple followers of the Lamb,
They lived, and spake, and thought the same!
Broke the commemorative bread,
And drank the Spirit of their Head.

3. On God they cast their every care,
Wrestling with God in mighty prayer
They claimed the grace through Jesus given,
By prayer they shut, and opened heaven.

4. To Jesus they performed their vows,
A little church in every house;
They joyfully conspired to raise
Their ceaseless sacrifice of praise.

5. Propriety was there unknown,
None called what he possessed his own:
Where all the common blessing share
No selfish happiness was there.

6. With grace abundantly endued,
A pure, believing multitude,
They all were of one heart and soul,
And only love inspired the whole.

7. O what an age of golden days!
O what a choice, peculiar race!
Washed in the Lamb's all-cleansing blood,
Anointed kings and priests to God!

8. Ye different sects, who all declare,
"Lo, here is Christ!" or, "Christ is there!"
Your stronger proofs divinely give,
And show me where the Christians live.

9. Join every soul that looks to Thee
In bonds of perfect charity;
Now, Lord, the glorious fullness give,
And all in all for ever live!

The shapes of the church to come 2 – varieties

Church within church within church . . .

Russian dolls fascinated me as a child. Whenever I saw them in a friend's toy box, on granny's mantelpiece or in a shop, I felt an irresistible desire to open them up and see how tiny the smallest one was and whether the detail was accurate.

The classic shapes of church remind me of those beautiful dolls. From an individual Christian, through a tiny intimate micro-church to the awe-inspiring macro-level, we should see Jesus wherever we look, each encompassing the other with Christ revealed in every part. Why, the very word "Christian" means "little Christ." The church is an amazing concept. Only God could think of such a plan!

Imagine the sounds emanating from Noah's Ark, with its eight human inhabitants and every species of animal. The whooping and laughter, the snorting and trumpeting as they realized they were safe and tumbled out into a cleansed earth to make a fresh start. Now it is tens of millions and creation itself which is being redeemed, set free to repossess the earth and occupy the heavens. What a celebration as we join "thousands upon thousands of angels in joyful assembly" (Hebrews 12:22). This is the church universal in rampant, extravagant worship, with Jesus at the centre of it all.

In Revelation 1 there's an amazing picture of Christ glorified. This description of Jesus is also a picture of his corporate body, for in Jesus we no longer live; he lives in us. We abide in him in heavenly places sharing his glory, and he abides in us on earth sharing our pain. So, church is Jesus alive and well in his people. When Paul speaks of church as the body of Christ it's not imagery – it's reality! No wonder when Jesus spoke, John heard "the sound of many waters" (Revelation 1:15 AV) a symbol of the many peoples and nations gathered into Jesus and shouting praise to him.

. . . wherever we look we see Jesus

As with our Russian dolls, if we open macro-church we find mega-church or city church across the earth mirroring something of heaven. If we unpack multi-church or local church, mini-church or house church and micro-church or cell church, they all will be visible representations of Jesus in some way.

Wherever we look we see Jesus, the greater dependent on the smaller for integrity (for the whole can only be as holy as its individual parts) and the smaller dependent on the greater for its visibility. Like the dolls, every individual expression of church has the same quality and character yet together we are one. However, the classic shapes of church are just one way to understand how we are being gathered. We must look further into scripture to discover the enormous variety in Christ and in church.

Team is church

I've already referred to *mobile-church*, as the first and only model of church Jesus left, but it is important enough to mention again. By raising up and endorsing his apostolic team as church, Jesus set a precedent for all time, one which we have ignored through history to our cost. We have marginalized the God-given missionary or growth forces within the church and labelled them *para-church*.

We evangelicals pride ourselves on our scriptural foundations and sound theology, but time and again we have missed the essence of what the Bible teaches about the most fundamental things. Nowhere in "The Book" do we find para-church, which means "beside church" or in the minds of some, "not really church." If para-church describes anything, it is the work of the Holy Spirit who comes alongside the church! The phrase has been conjured up to keep at bay those who seem to threaten what possessive and sometimes hierarchical church leaders have come to regard as their domain. In God's eyes there's only church. Para-church really is church too.

Church is God's secret weapon, his master plan, conceived before time. He recognizes nothing else. We box and tie up the apostolic evangelists because they challenge and shake our structures and tidy minds. They stir our people with visions of the lost on our doorstep and at the ends of the earth, and that's exactly what God sent them to do. They are church at the cutting edge, yet some have said, "If you want our (meagre) support, go play evangelistic games elsewhere, don't interfere on our patch."

In doing this we elevate our pastoral gift and alienate the very ones who can help us build. We have set in place a pattern for decline. What a deception! What kind of being takes the life force within its own body and keeps it from performing the function for which it was designed?

Apostolic evangelists must stir us and help plant churches in every street of every town. All we should ask is that they respect what exists and work together in the joys and challenges of building. Some will have a deal of repenting to do when, in the kingdom, we face the likes of George Verwer, founder of Operation Mobilization; Loren Cunningham, Youth With a Mission; Billy Graham, Youth For Christ, and thousands of unknown ministries and teams misunderstood and hindered in their work for Jesus.

All things to all men

Every group of believers gathered by Jesus is church, whatever shape or form, be it local or mobile. The possibilities for fresh models of church are endless. True apostles, with their passion for growth, will be creative, not bound by traditional concepts, or by current "New Church" models, good in their time but some well past their sell-by-date. They will not keep trying to get people to church, but will take church to the people in Jesus-style, incarnational, church-planting. We haven't improved on his way yet, Paul called it, becoming "all things to all men so that by all possible means I might save some" (1 Corinthians 9:22).

In *Changing World Changing Church*, Dr Moynagh underlines this concept:

> Becoming sensitive to the different mindsets of work and leisure would be a step away from a one-size-fits-all approach to evangelism. Church would have begun to leave standardisation behind; it would be reaching out to the it-must-fit-me world. Instead of dragging people at work to us, church would start going to them. It would be church that fits – not just those who've come in, but those who are currently outside.

Let me give you an extraordinary example of taking church to the people. In 1990 Lynn Green, a YWAM director in the UK, began to research the idea of a reconciliation walk along the old Crusade route from Cologne to Jerusalem. Two young men turned out of Israel suggested it and at first Lynn rejected the idea. Later the Lord spoke to him and the plan unfolded. The walk of repentance, to seek forgiveness for our churches' historic crimes against Muslims and Jews, was the result.

Lynn speaks of amazing responses as the team travelled with genuine humility and no hidden agenda to convert their hearers. With honest statements of repentance, acknowledging our sins as representatives of Christ, they sought to right the wrongs of the past. They made startling discoveries – God has been at work in the hearts of many Muslims who do not share the strong fundamentalist views of terrorist extremists who hit the headlines. To Lynn's surprise he found a deep spirituality among some key leaders, who also declared a firm belief in Jesus. Their lifestyles often reflected more of Christ than much of what we call Christianity in the West.

No favouritism

Lynn remembered Peter's experience at the house of Cornelius. Obeying the Spirit, Peter went against his rigid upbringing and tradition, reaching beyond his understanding and risking rejection by fellow Jewish believers. When God blessed he willingly confessed, "I now realize how true it is that God does not show favouritism but accepts men from every nation who fear him and do what is right" (Acts 10:34–35).

Time will reveal what Lynn and his faithful band accomplished. They crossed a major threshold and took the true spirit of church to a people of whom some would be deeply suspicious. Only God's genius and yielded leadership could achieve this – Lynn is an apostle. The first Imam to hear the reconciliation message declared, "the man who conceived this idea had an epiphany (a visitation) from God." He was right!

Sequel

In 1998 the press in the UK carried an interesting story. The Pope, reflecting on the weaknesses of the Roman Catholic Church over the last 2,000 years, asked for a document to be prepared outlining a response to these failures as a beginning to the new millennium. He spoke of "purifying memories" through repentance, and the Crusades were specifically mentioned. Is it possible that Lynn's act of obedience caused these stirrings in the Vatican? We'll never know, but it's incredible that such things are taking place at this particular time in history.

Today we respect Jewish Christians who take the name "Messianic Jews" and maintain much of their culture. Should we not also afford Muslim people, who turn to Jesus, the same privilege? I expect a new movement of "Messianic Muslims" to emerge with a strong moral edge and an unerring love for Jesus (London Bible College's Islamic Centre confirms this is already happening). Since Peter visited Cornelius the world has become our parish. No people on earth are beyond the reach of God's love. Church can break out in every culture and network of humanity. There's no defence against love; its power is supreme.

Church planting in people groups

In the New Testament we see incredible advance for the gospel through church-planting by apostles and saints, often dispersed through persecution. Churches sprang up across Jerusalem, Judea and Samaria, as Jesus commanded (Acts 1:8). There were Jewish churches, Samaritan churches and Gentile churches, often existing side by side with blessing and conflict to encourage and test the leaders.

These homogeneous churches, planted among different people groups, from rebellious Cretans to God-fearing Greeks and diligent Bereans, are seen throughout Acts and the Epistles – encouraged to meet in the context of their culture and language, but also taking their place in the body of Christ as a whole. If, for example, a white middle-class, or a black Nigerian church is not seeking to serve and co-operate with other churches, they'd either be extremely immature or plainly disobedient. Revelation 7:9 clearly describes a united gathering of distinct people and language groups, standing as one great assembly to worship Jesus.

The churches in Judea, Galilee and Samaria are referred to as "the church" (Acts 9:31), as were believers meeting in a home (Colossians 4:15). The New Testament writers were not confused, but understood the Jewish concepts of absolute and composite unity. For example, each piece of a loaf is bread (not breads); it has the same characteristics as the whole, also bread (1 Corinthians 10:17). Similarly each member of the Godhead is God, the three are God, not Gods. There is only God; there is only bread; there is only church; we cannot separate the parts from the whole.

The shortest word for God in Hebrew is "EL," but on its own the letter "Shin," like our "E", with its three strokes joined as one symbolizes the Trinity. This letter, embroidered on phylacteries worn by Jews at morning prayer, and engraved on the casings of their doorposts, is a constant reminder that the Lord is the ultimate expression of composite and absolute unity.

Kensington Temple Elim Church in London, England, is a great picture of absolute and composite unity. Under the leadership of Wynne Lewis and latterly Colin Dye, 120 satellite churches have been planted in and around London. Fourteen are homogeneous people groups, initially drawn together using the language and food of the different cultures. Such diversity, yet the many expressions are one church. So, Nigerian church, Filipino church, Chinese church and so on, are all part of the 6,000-strong mega-church with 110 nationalities that makes "KT" what it is.

Concerning food, Martin Scott points out, before we preach the gospel, as a means of identifying with people, Jesus commanded "eat what is set before you" (Luke 10:8). The way we give and receive food is an important part of our mission strategy. Hit-and-run evangelism is difficult. The incarnational approach relates to unreached people through homes and hospitality, not just hotels and videos. The common meal instigated by Jesus lost the power of its simplicity as a family and friends affair as Simson underlines in *Houses that Change the World*. Under the heading 'The end of the Lord's Supper,' he says:

Since it is quite difficult to feed a cathedral full of people with real food, it (the Lord's Supper) degenerated into a religious and symbolic ritual, offering microscopic sips of wine and a small wafer ...
As biblical commentator William Barclay writes: "The celebration of the Lord's Supper in a Christian home in the first century and in

a cathedral in the twentieth century cannot be more different, they bear no relationship to one another whatsoever."

Many and varied shapes

We also see other homogeneous churches in scripture which are not simply ethnic in origin. For instance, there were groupings of Grecian and Hebraic widows (Acts 6:1): could these be *generational church*? When the elderly, infirm or young can't meet with the rest of the church, the principle of planting church where they are must apply. In Pioneer People, it is our goal to plant churches in schools, homes for the elderly and also among disabled people.

Antioch was an *international church* with people of many races – Jews, Cypriots, Cyreneans and Greeks are mentioned (Acts 13). It was also a resource church, sending the cream of its leadership to serve elsewhere. In Caesar's household there was a gathering (Philippians 4:22), quite possibly a *slaves' church*. Paul began in Ephesus in the school of Tyrannus (Acts 19:9). For two years this was a *teaching centre church* and all who lived in Asia heard the word of the Lord.

Towards the end of his ministry Paul hosted church whilst awaiting trial in Rome – *prison church*? In our own area we have run Alpha courses in a prison, during which the team saw over 50 give their lives to Jesus – a real cell church!

Stories from South American revivals tell of whole prisons, originally in the grip of crime syndicates, being turned over to the church that has developed inside them. The success of these prison churches has led the authorities to institute their own church-planting scheme by transferring Christian prisoners to other prisons to repeat the process. In the UK an Anglican prison chaplain was given a grant from funds to visit South America to learn and apply the principles here in Britain.

The homes of Cornelius, a centurion (Acts 10:1), and Lydia,

a businesswoman (Acts 16:14), no doubt attracted particular segments of the community producing a flavour of their own. I see the benefits of a *military campus church* on, say, an American army base in the UK, or a *business people's church* in a large company, providing these groups also co-operate wherever possible with the wider body of Christians. Roger Ellis, leader of a resource church in the Pioneer network, has started a cell church movement in universities. "Fusion" provides the resources for many new cells which in time could give place to strong expressions of *university church*.

Youth church initiatives are taking church into the heart of clubland and the red light districts of some major cities. Thousands of British gypsies have been converted in recent years, giving rise to *gypsy churches*. One such church, near my home, was asked by the council if they would like to name the road leading to their site – they called it "Salvation Place." Since the introduction of Sunday trading in England at least two groups, instead of moaning, have sought to plant in Tesco superstores (Publix in the USA) with the management's blessing! Why not *superstore churches*?

In *We Dance Because We Cannot Fly* (Marshall Pickering), Guy Chevreaux tells the amazing story of Betel. WEC missionary Elliot Tepper stumbled on a radical expression of church, exactly what the drug addicts of Spain needed to help them kick the habit and find Jesus. So successful are these *ex-addict churches* they have spread to 110 centres, in 50 metropolitan areas of nine countries and growing . . .

From Nigeria I heard of an *ex-AIDS church* – to join you must have medical evidence to show you had AIDS and the same to prove you've been healed! Youth For Christ in Britain have a chat room on their website where teenagers chat, ask questions and receive advice from the "pastor" – is this *cyber church*?

The great church breakout

Church without walls means that as the Holy Spirit broke out of heaven to come to us, we break out of our ghettos to take church wherever people are. Church in the leisure centre, surgery, and hospital; church in the orchestra, football league and theatre; church in parliament, airport and factory. Even some of our "churches" where the lamp of spirituality dimmed long ago, might be revitalized to become church again. Indeed, the cathedrals in Britain are filling up, and many attending are young people looking for God in liturgy, symbolism and the beauty of those old buildings.

You may ask, with all this diversity, where's unity gone? Michael Moynagh, in *Changing World, Changing Church* says, "Connected fragments were the essence of the New Testament Church." I see it like a downpour of rain. First the hard ground absorbs the drops, then pools form in the dips. If rain persists the pools widen and deepen and slowly merge, until they become one great lake. Most people need the security of a familiar group. As we mature, we learn to sacrifice and reach out without losing our identity and distinctives.

Strangely the older, supposedly more mature Christians become inflexible and fixed in their ways, expecting others to adapt to them. Does this mean that many who have been Christians for years have never really grown up? Paul's cry in 1 Corinthians 9:20–23, calls for established saints to adapt for the newcomer and the unreached. The church must become a "house of prayer for *all* nations," a meeting place for *all* peoples and cultures where everyone is valued and given their place.

Our English word "university" can be read as comprising two words, "unity" and "diversity" which should describe the church. Indeed, we should see ourselves as a place of learning – "university of God" might be a good name for the church.

Hopefully we will increasingly express these qualities and release people from the opposite bondages of conformity and division.

Jubilee

Jubilee in our society is associated with fiftieth anniversary celebrations, but its origin is in scripture. Virtually the whole of Leviticus chapter 25 records the instructions the Lord gave to Moses concerning the "Year of Jubilee." Jubilee literally means "time of shouting," when debts were cancelled, property returned, slaves released and the land rested. Like much in the Old Testament it was a signpost pointing to the day when Christ comes to establish his kingdom and set captives free. Sadly, it was never practised in Israel's history. The nearest thing to Jubilee was in the early church where no one counted anything as being their own and no one had any need (Acts 4:32).

At a gathering of church leaders Christine and I are working with, I asked Neil Edbrook from Bristol Christian Fellowship to speak briefly on the subject of church. At first I was disappointed when he talked about church as a wedding! As he warmed to his theme, I realized he was on to something special. A wedding is an event with a purpose. It has all the elements of life, food and drink, friends, guests, celebration and commitment, and into this Jesus came to perform his first miracle, unlike some of our gatherings with no real purpose, little content and where Jesus rarely seems to turn up. The more I thought about Jesus' ministry and that of the apostles, the more I saw they centred on life events where food, excitement, teaching and the supernatural blended in a way that provoked conviction, curiosity, enquiry, amazement and worship.

Those early chapters of Acts were a foretaste of what's to come. They demonstrated the norm among God's people. New and diverse expressions of church born of God will also manifest the Spirit of Jubilee. In fact, Jubilee practised will supersede the need for new ways of being church, such will be the blessings of the lifestyle that many dispossessed, marginalized and poor will flock to join. Israel too will be made envious (Romans 11:11) as Gentile believers enjoy the benefits of a festival first given to Jews. Perhaps they'll join the party too – please God!

Marks of maturity

As I close this chapter let me focus our attention on two other shapes, or rather qualities, of church we see emerging among God's people around the world. They are signs of maturity. The first is *married-church*, church devoted to Jesus the Lamb and aiming to follow him wherever he goes. Wedded to his will, she puts aside her own interest to please her Lord as a bride, ready for a permanent relationship with the bridegroom coming to make her his own.

The second is related and precedes the first. It is *martyr church*. The highest honour we can know is to share the fellowship of Christ's sufferings. We don't ask to suffer any more than Jesus did but those who do mostly count it joy. Only grace can achieve this. So the world gets an understanding of what Jesus did on the cross as they see saints willing to sacrifice and even die for their faith. This may be the last great act of the church, Christ's body on earth, laying down her life for the one she loves. This final offering will bring history's greatest harvest as the dying love of Jesus is seen, this time in his people (Revelation 11:7–11).

CHAPTER 17

THE CHURCH AND THE DESTINY OF THE NATIONS

Signs of the times

Earthquake activity is one of the signs Jesus said would mark the approach of the end of the age, along with national strife and famine. After this, waves of hatred and persecution would be directed towards his followers and their faith would be severely tested. Increased wickedness, false prophets and deception would abound, with the love of many Christians growing cold under the pressures (Matthew 24:11–12).

Earthquakes raise great interest among the "prophets." Do current statistics indicate an upward trend or not? Figures vary amazingly from no significant change, to massive increase, and they need interpreting. Do we mean the really big boys or simply any old quake? Do we take into account more accurate records in recent years? In terms of the number of deaths, have we taken population growth into account?

Surfing the Net seems to reveal a fairly large rise during the 1990s over the 1980s, the monthly average of quakes over 6.5 on the Richter scale was 52 during the nineties as opposed to

36 during the eighties. The year 1995 saw 75, the greatest number since 1973. However, earthquakes were much in the news at the close of the millennium, with tragic pictures constantly on our screens.

Looking at climate generally, there is a growing concern about the extremes we experience, with global warming, El Niño and holes in the ozone layer, variously held responsible. Without doubt, we're seeing many of the signs Jesus predicted coming to pass, but he warned us not to be taken in by these. At best, they only point towards the major confirmation he gave concerning the timing of the end of this age.

With all these dark clouds of evil gathering, the promise in Matthew 24:14 shines as a searchlight of hope across skies of gloom – "this gospel of the kingdom will be preached in the whole world as a testimony to all nations, and then the end will come." We mustn't focus on darkness engulfing our world, but on the glorious promise that, under great duress, the people of God will complete the task Jesus entrusted to us.

So, creation groans in the agony of her final labour pains which, if there were no assurance of a birth, would leave us in despair. However, deep in our hearts, we Christians know the final outcome of the drama. This is not a phantom pregnancy or a stillbirth. No! Together with the angels and all creation, we stand on tiptoe expectantly, waiting for the "sons" of God to claim their inheritance in Christ (Romans 8:22–23). A primary part of this inheritance we share with Jesus, is "the nations", the peoples to whom we have been sent all over the world (Psalm 2:8). This ingathering is the answer to the prayer Jesus taught us to pray with hope, "your kingdom come, your will be done *on earth* as it is in heaven" (Matthew 6:10, my italics).

Focus planet earth

While our escapist mentality looks for heaven, the Lord keeps his eye on earth. When Jesus returns, to take the government of the globe on his shoulders, "the meek . . . will inherit *the earth*" (Matthew 5:5, my italics). His kingdom rule will be visibly established and the humble will share responsibility with him. How so many Christians have missed this basic truth is a mystery hard to comprehend. The idea the church will be whisked away to some distant, heavenly space station is foreign to scripture.

I repeat, Jesus called us to pray "your kingdom come, your will be done *on earth* as it is in heaven" (Matthew 6:10, my italics). Earth is where the final action takes place. Earth is where the spiritual and physical realms, blown apart by sin, are reunited. Jesus began this work of reconciliation 2,000 years ago, and created the church to spread this good news about the kingdom of God. Understanding this reality and experiencing the thrill of anticipation led many in New Churches to confuse church and kingdom in our early days. This was the reason some accused us of triumphalism.

Whilst such confusion was not excusable, it was understandable as the church lives with incredible tension. On the one hand is the excitement of kingdom among us, yet at the same time, there's frustration knowing it is still to come. Our objective is to see God's kingdom visibly established in our physical world. The church is the vehicle God is using to bring this about, and nations responding to the rule and reign of Jesus are the result and the inheritance promised to the saints.

Nation against nation

So, tribes and peoples of the earth are very much on God's heart, central to his plan. For this reason they must also be the main focus of the church. Our future is wrapped up with their response to the gospel. It's not surprising then, at this important time in history, that violence and aggression between nations is escalating. Satan is stirring nation against nation in a last attempt to foil God's plans for harvest. Sadly, the church has often remained silent about or actually blessed or, worse still, participated in the conflicts. This is not the place to discuss "just war," but we might do well to examine the understanding of those who advocate "peace churches."

Since the collapse of communism we have seen a significant rise in aggression between peoples. In 1997 there were 24 armed conflicts within countries and only one between geographically defined nations, the latter between Pakistan and India. In six years the total cost of war in Bosnia topped $48 billion and tens of thousands of lives were senselessly terminated. What happened in Kosovo goes way beyond this, and the war against terrorism will make these amounts seem like pocket money. Why after decades of at least partial peace are old wounds opening once more to cause such pain again? Why, after experiencing the two worst wars in history, have we not learned the lessons of peace and reconciliation? Why are the tribes of the earth still hell bent on exterminating one another? The answer is two-fold – identity and land.

Identity and land

Every individual, family, group and tribe cries like an orphan child, "Who am I?" and "Where is my home?" There's not a war which does not have one, or both, of these questions at its root. They come from strength, as with Hitler towards Jewish people, "We are superior to you; get out of our land!" or from weakness as with, say, the Kurds in Iraq or the Albanians in Serbia,

"Please help us, we too have a name and a right to somewhere to live!"

As global uniformity closes around us, our family name and a place to live become more important to us all. Whether it's Northern Ireland or North Korea, an Aborigine or a Zionist, the quest is for recognition and territory and sometimes for control. Christians must learn when to uphold a people's identity for their welfare and protection, and when to challenge it to underline the kingdom principle that there is neither Jew nor Greek. Perhaps the strength or weakness of the people concerned will help us determine the approach.

The promised land

The Middle East is particularly relevant in this connection today. Jews claim the land through Abraham by Isaac; Arabs claim it through Abraham by Ishmael; Christians claim Abraham as father through Christ and sought to possess the land by Crusade. Each of us argues over particular sites of importance to our faith or denomination. So Jerusalem has become a focus for violence and a symbol of division. It is physical evidence that God is with none of us in our quarrels and killing.

So, who has the right to that tiny piece of land, the centre of so much controversy where the eyes of the world are fixed?

As the first church was almost entirely Jewish and devoted to Jesus, we could say this original persecuted Christian minority retained, or better, obtained, a right to the land promised to Abraham's descendants. There's no question that God has brought the Jews back to Israel in fulfillment of prophecy and in order to deal with them in the context of their home and history. But, true though this is, we must look to the future they, and all peoples, have in Christ, rather than to the past to recapture what was only a signpost anyway. The future will restore the best of Jewish life with its colour, community, extended family, intimacy and humour, but added will be the "Jesus" dimension of grace, truth, freedom and holiness. For, if God does not keep his promises to the Jews, how can we be sure he will keep his promises to us Gentiles?

Abraham – key to unity . . .

I will come back to the question of who has rights to the land. First let me share an experience which helped me understand the importance of land. The Lord had been speaking about reconciliation between Britain and Germany, two countries responsible for so much hurt in recent history. My belief is that, through repentance and commitment to one another, God will use us together to model something fresh in those nations we have abused.

My journey in this respect moved from passive acceptance of Germans after the Lord dealt with a residue of racism deposited in me during the war years. Loren Cunningham, founder of Youth With a Mission, encouraged us to rescue the Christian heritage of Germany and see it as a signpost pointing to their destiny, and that helped me take another giant step. Germany gave us the printed Bible, a hundred years of prayer, the Reformation and modern missionary movement. This godly history must be the foundation for their future.

I was attending a small gathering of European leaders in Frankfurt. The Lord prompted me to lie outstretched on the floor. I was not simply to ask God for a love for German people, but also for their land. The tears flowed and my body heaved; something happened in my heart as I realized there's been an inextricable link between people and land since creation. God made it that way. But that was not all that took place. A seed of revelation dropped into my heart.

There in the place where anti-semitism once thrived, I heard, "Abraham is the key to unity among Muslims, Jews and Christians!" I didn't, and still don't, understand what this means. I just know that we are about to see an unprecedented breaking down of barriers between sections of the three major monotheistic religions, as the Lord shows us how to apply this truth. It will have something to do with love for land, respect for one another and rejection of grabbing and violence to obtain territory.

... and land

There is a strong connection between people and land in both Old and New Testaments, whether it be Israel inheriting the promised land or the meek inheriting the earth. God's original purpose for mankind to "rule over" creation (Genesis 1:26) has not changed. Therefore the health of humanity is linked to the health of land and the redemption of mankind is linked to the redemption of creation. Martin Scott in *Sowing Seeds For Revival* (Sovereign World), makes this observation:

> God brings Israel into a covenant and this covenant includes a promise of land, but when they sin they lose the land that they have been promised. Although the land had been promised to them for "all generations," as a result of their sin they find that they become separated from their Promised Land. The dislocation means they go into exile as the land becomes sick and vomits them out (Leviticus 18:28). Hence as the people humble themselves and intercede there is the possibility of the land being healed. 2 Chronicles 7:14 does not say that God will heal the people in

response to their repentance but that the land will be healed. I suggest that the very process of repentance brings healing to the people, but the promise of God is to bring healing at a deeper level. Could it be in some revivals that people are healed but the land remains sick? Perhaps when land is not healed we can reap a harvest for a season, but then the land returns to its former state, causing a premature termination to the season of fruitfulness.

All nations blessed

Ephesians 1 reminds us it was always God's purpose to "bring all things in heaven and on earth together under one head, even Christ" (v.10). The promise to bless nations was given to Abraham and Sarah individually and also repeated to Isaac, so there is no doubt what God intended. "In you Abraham, in you Sarah and in you Isaac, I will bless all nations," (Genesis 17:4 & 16 and 26:4; Galatians 3:8–9): the Lord reiterated his covenant over and over again.

God never called Abraham to be father to Jewish people alone (Romans 4:16–17). From the beginning he was the father of the faithful in all nations, demonstrated by including Gentile women in the lineage of Jesus. By jealously seeking to guard their ancient heritage, the Jews temporarily lost it as faith was always necessary for a relationship with the patriarch and his God, as it is today. Before Abraham was, Jesus existed (John 8:58); he invaded our world as a man to help us find our destiny of blessing in Abraham, father of all nations. Scripture shows us God's love for the world and its inhabitants and that he has a plan for every individual, family, tribe and nation on the earth, Israel included.

We're not here as fodder for any mad dictator who may pass by, nor are we playthings for the devil or some remote god, lonely and bored with his own presence. We were made for friendship, as children, with our Father God, our Abba, Daddy, and Jesus Christ, our elder brother, designed to share his nature and to live in a loving relationship with him forever.

The whole earth filled

Now to my earlier question, who has a right to the land God promised Abraham? The answer is clear. The meek from all nations, including Israel, who, in Christ, will inherit the earth, will also possess this little piece of the Middle East. God begins with the lesser to achieve the greater. He began with one family, Abraham's, to bless all families, with one day, the Sabbath, to bring a millennium of rest. Jacob's stone at Bethel (house of God) led to Solomon's Temple and now to a house of living stones. God began with Canaan, but will end with the whole earth in the hands of the redeemed. Jerusalem will be the jewel, not as a decaying city of purely archaeological interest but as a living, blood-washed bride.

The progression is from the signpost to the goal. The goal does not mean the signpost was wrong, simply obsolete when we arrive. So a small piece of land ends with the earth filled with God's glory. That land is still the signpost pointing to our destination and, until we arrive, it will be an important focus of attention and events. However, God's children from the nations do not look back hoping for the restoration of a few square miles, but forward to the day when every inch of the planet will be given to God's people to occupy and enjoy.

Knowing this, and discovering God's love for the people of Britain in spite of past weaknesses, gives me a love for all other tribes of the earth. I have a growing passion to help downtrodden peoples find their identity and purpose in Jesus. The prophets saw this and longed for the day when all families would live in peace and harmony. Isaiah cried out on God's behalf, "Turn to me and be saved, all you ends of the earth; for I am God, and there is no other . . . Before me every knee will bow; by me every tongue will swear" (45:22–23). Jeremiah prophesied a time when "all nations will gather in Jerusalem to honour the name of the Lord" (3:17). Ezekiel saw the new temple which features so powerfully in John's revelation where, on the banks of the river which flows from this house, grows the tree whose leaves are for the healing of the nations (Revelation 22:2).

Imagine the jubilant scenes as all strife subsides in the wake of the good news reaching every dark corner of the globe. Just think of the unspeakable joy as violence, hatred and aggression melt away in the presence of God's royal Prince of Peace. The differences between us, which caused fear and uncertainty, now blend together in a glorious array of perfume, colour, sound and dance as we worship and cry, "Salvation belongs to our God, who sits on the throne, and to the Lamb" (Revelation 7:10).

The power of the blood

So, God's solution to ethnic problems is cleansing, not through eradication but through washing in the blood of Jesus. His blood is effective, not only for me and my family but for all the peoples of the world. Great psalmists of the modern missionary movements of the last century saw this and expressed it in hymns. The *Primitive Methodist Hymnal* compiled in 1882 has these words by Professor Saunderson:

> When shall that sound of gladness,
> Our hills and vales along,
> The Jew recall from sadness,
> The Moslem wake to song?
> When shall each heathen nation,
> Renouncing idol fanes,

> In prostrate adoration,
> Acknowledge Jesus reigns?

Not, perhaps, the finest poetry, but the vision is immaculate. William Booth, a latter-day apostle who raised an army for God, wrote:

> O boundless salvation! Deep ocean of love,
> O fullness of mercy, Christ brought from above,
> The whole world redeeming, so rich and so free,
> Now flowing for all men, come, roll over me!

If it's true God's love for people was so great he gave his most treasured possession to salvage a lost world, how can the church, called to reflect that love, do less? It's our joy to give our best to participate in redemption strategy. Touched by the compassion of God that released his Son to the cross, we too will gladly lay down our lives, careers, money, children, and preferences – to serve his great and glorious cause.

May the church rise to the call of the Spirit and accept the challenge to carry the news that Jesus is alive and well across every mountain range and ocean until people are worshipping Jesus in every one of the 6,700 languages and thousands more dialects spoken in the world today.

CHAPTER 18

THE CHURCH AND THE DESTINY OF ISRAEL

Controversy and conflict

Our journey in the New Churches over the last 35 years has not been without dispute. Law and grace, the role of women in leadership, the nature of church, discipleship, apostolic ministry, prophecy and creativity have all produced controversy. However, few subjects have stirred as much reaction as that of the place of Israel in the purposes of God. This is not surprising as the Jews have been the centre of attention through centuries, hated by many and almost worshipped by some. Still they are the focus of the media, and nations are divided concerning their future.

These divisions are reflected in attitudes which exist among Christians, emotions run high and blind our minds to reason and healthy discussion. Some feel so passionately about this people and their land that they believe the Jews can do no wrong and Palestinian aggression only confirms their belief. On the other hand, those who favour an Arab perspective, aware of the injustices perpetrated by Israel, are labelled anti-semitic, which is strange as both Jews and Arabs are descended from Shem!

At the heart of the conflict is the belief, in the three major monotheistic religions, that their brand of faith is the true light and should dominate the world. Islamic, Zionist and Christian groups really believe that the world rightfully belongs to them and they should control its future. Whilst the moderates can live at peace with their neighbours, trusting the almighty to bring about his will, the zealots feel bound to help God by whatever means they can.

And this is not just an Arab/Israeli problem. In the USA particularly there are right-wing, evangelical, reconstructionist groups who believe Christians should be running the world. Some of these would take up arms to defend their freedom and right to promote their objectives. Christian history is littered with failed examples of the rich and powerful mistakenly believing that it is possible to force the masses to faith. Even our best missionary efforts were tainted with paternalism. It's amazing how God used them in spite of this.

Redeeming power

Tom Marshall, known for writings and teaching on leadership and relationships, spoke about power and power abuse. He underlined the fact that wrong use of power leads to loss of power, demonstrated through the collapse of every great civilization, empire and ideology. He reminded us that Jesus humbled himself and came as a man to redeem power through sacrifice, the opposite of every worldly authority.

An insignificant Nazarene confronted religious, military and political powers in weakness, as a lamb before its shearers, and overcame (Isaiah 53:7). Through his atoning death he began the process that will lead to his enthronement on earth as King of kings and Lord of lords. By his example the vicious cycle of the oppressed becoming the oppressor, with history repeating itself, is broken, and love triumphs.

The original church was, of course, Jewish and the threat of the imposition of Jewish culture and tradition on new Gentile Christians was real. Paul's tenacity and determination kept the gospel pure. Now the church, dominated by Western culture, is seeing the reverse of what happened in those early days. Jewish people, and those of other faiths who are turning to Christ, are pressurized to give up their culture. This has caused unnecessary and tragic divisions between converts and their families.

Messianic Christians . . .

Today many people see Christianity as synonymous with immorality, Western imperialism and aggression, and it is impossible for some to adopt the term "Christian" at all. So, we have "Messianic Jews" and the possibility of "Messianic Muslims." Perhaps, as the Gentile church is renewed, we will have "Messianic Christians" as well! This could be a welcome alternative to "born-again Christian" which some have used to disassociate themselves from nominalism. Now, even the term "born-again" is linked with right-wing fundamentalism in certain places.

Whatever we do we mustn't confuse Christianity and culture. A masterstroke of the enemy muddied the waters of the stream of God's new life by merging state and church and giving us "Christian nations." There is no Christian nation, nor is there Christian culture. Jesus came to purify our cultures and bind them together in a complex, multi-coloured church full of beauty and diversity.

. . . in a truly catholic church?

Naturally, there is much in every culture which is abhorrent, but equally there is much which comes from the creative heart placed within us by our heavenly Father. We must release this creativity which exists in all peoples, and then a truly catholic church will emerge which answers Jesus' prayer in John 17 "that they may be one . . . to let the world know that you sent me" (v.22–23).

Jesus prophesied this coming together of peoples from all points of the compass to take their places at the feast in the kingdom of God (Luke 13:29). Song-writer Martin Smith and Delirious? echo this:

> Shout to the north and the south,
> Sing to the east and the west:
> "Jesus is saviour to all,
> Lord of heaven and earth."
>> Martin Smith © 1995, Curious Music UK,
>> by kind permission of Furious? Records

Hundreds of years ago the prophets foresaw a time when the nations would stream to Mount Zion to walk in the light of God's city and bring their wealth to adorn it (Isaiah 60:1–6, Psalm 48, etc). What a day when Jews and Arabs sit down together with Western nations, no hidden agenda and no hatred or animosity. Only at the cross do we meet as equals on level ground.

The importance of Hebron

In a TV news bulletin during strife between the Israelis and Palestinians, an interviewer quizzed an Israeli soldier about Hebron. He asked why there was so much concern over the area. The soldier answered, giving no explanation that, in some ways, Hebron was more important than Jerusalem to Jews. As I pondered this I was reminded that Hebron was the place where David united the previously divided tribes, where together they carried him back to Jerusalem to install him as king over Israel and Judah.

The symbolism of Hebron is important for Gentiles too. Hebron means "a company" and speaks of companionship and solidarity. Now great David's greater Son is uniting all tribes of the earth in peace. From our spiritual Hebron we will march, as a company, to our heavenly "Jerusalem" and crown Jesus Lord of all.

Heaven to earth

The biblical concept of an alternative nation to Israel was emphasized by New Churches as an antidote to misinterpretation of prophecies concerning the place of Israel in the end times. To put it simply, there were Christians who believed that the church would be "raptured" or whisked away from earth by the Spirit. What remained of Israel would go through tribulation. Thus purged in fires of suffering, they would complete the work of witnessing to the nations in a dark and difficult time.

This view defeats the reason for Jesus coming to establish his kingdom on earth with people from every tribe and tongue. We're not going to heaven; heaven is coming to earth! Jesus' references to things being as they were in the days of Noah and to two people working in a field, one being taken, the other left (Luke 17:26–37), along with other scriptures, are used to support the "rapture" theory. However, after the flood it was Noah who remained to repopulate the world – the wicked were removed!

I'm not attempting to answer all the questions this raises. Unanswered questions are healthy and something we Christians must live with as God unfolds his plan. The full understanding of prophecy is revealed in the event. Questions are evidence we are still seekers, and striving to understand God's heart and mind. We should be wary of those who claim to have all the answers and whatever answers we have must be in harmony with the centrality of the death and resurrection of Jesus and his purpose for the world and its peoples. All prophecy and scripture must be interpreted in the light of these key events of history.

Jesus clearly stated that the kingdom would be taken from the Jews and given to "a *nation* bringing forth the fruits" (Matthew 21:43, AV, my italics). Peter underlined this, likening the church to a living temple calling us, not only a holy nation, but also a chosen people and a royal priesthood (1 Peter 2:9). He took the language of Zion and applied it to the church. Did this mean God had given up on Israel, rejecting them in favour of the new Gentile church?

Replacement . . .

Such a belief has been attributed to the New Churches. However, the accusation that we all subscribe to "replacement theology" will not stick. Mind you, if we are truly evangelical we must believe in, at least, fulfillment theology. Only the most fanatical Israel restorationists anticipate the rebuilding of a literal temple, with a revived Levitical priesthood, offering animal sacrifices to atone for the sins of the nation. There couldn't be a greater abomination to God and insult to his Son who gave his life to fulfil this old covenant symbolism and become the substance of its shadow.

Jesus fulfilled the law (Matthew 5:17) which, although good, had no power to save, only to condemn. That law, together with the ordinances and the old covenant, are now declared obsolete, defunct and out of date, in the light of all Jesus accomplished (Romans 10:4/Hebrews 8:13). We have a new law, the law of the Spirit of life (Romans 8:2), and this royal law of love reigns (James 2:8). Jesus is the slain Lamb; we need no other.

Those justified by faith in his substitutional death are washed in his blood and become a new royal priestly order. They are built into a temple as a permanent dwelling for God.

Some theologians, outside the New Churches, would argue that *Jesus* was into "replacement." He replaced Israel not with the Gentile church, but with a new Israel out of the nation itself. The Israel of old replaced by a new Israel from within – an all Jewish replacement to boot! The 12 apostles replacing the patriarchs, Jesus replacing the Passover lamb and a Jewish church or a living Jewish temple replacing the old building. It's true the first church was completely Jewish and Jews played a key role until they were finally driven out of the church in AD 325 by Constantine at the council of Nicea. Not that I subscribe to this view, but it's an interesting perspective. So where does all this leave Israel?

. . . or inclusion theology?

Rather than using "replacement" to describe what most people in the New Churches believe concerning Israel, I prefer to use "inclusion." "Inclusion theology" represents what scripture has to say on this matter. It also expresses what was in God's mind long before he called Abraham and promised to bless all people through him.

An important key to understanding what the Bible says about the destiny of Israel and her relationship to the church is found in Romans 9–11. Here, Paul explains that, like the branch of an olive tree, Israel was cut off from her roots when she rejected her Messiah. However, the Lord is a master at bringing good out of evil and the rejection of Jesus by the Jewish leadership cleared the way for the gospel to be taken to the Gentile nations. From that point in history the term "chosen people" had to be completely redefined.

Only one root

With one snip of the divine secateurs the master-gardener cut away a natural olive branch from the root and lovingly grafted on to the *same root* a wild branch. Note, the wild branch was grafted on to the *same root* stock, not a different one. "Abraham believed God, and it was credited to him as righteousness" (James 2:23). Thus he became father of *all* the faithful. Now by faith in Jesus, the spiritual seed of Abraham, the children of promise are regarded as his offspring.

If God can bring such blessing out of rejection, what can he do with acceptance? If we Gentiles have been included in God's plan for the world as a result of Israel's transgression, what kind of blessing will we receive when Israel, through repentance, is grafted back into the root from which it was taken – the same root? Obviously, this result will lead to the culmination of all things, the glorious finale which we have all been eagerly awaiting. That's "inclusion theology!"

The Jews are coming home!

It is starting to happen. Jewish people are beginning to recognize Jesus their Messiah. I relish the picture. Angels leaning over the balcony of heaven, straining to make sense of the sounds. Shouts of joy coming from earth at the same time as deep sobbing and repentance. The crunch of boots on gravel paths as numbers join in the march towards the New Jerusalem. Screams of excitement, the noise of running feet.

The intercessors, faithfully watching and praying, are the first to realize what's going on. Their long vigil is over, their supplications turn to thanksgiving. Grunts, sounds of snapping twigs in the scramble to take down harps from willow trees. "We're going home! Don't you see, at last we're going home?"

The psalmist saw it and the old 1611 translation captured the true meaning:

> When the Lord turned again the captivity of Zion,
> we were like them that dream.
> Then was our mouth filled with laughter,
> and our tongue with singing:
> then said they among the heathen,
> The Lord hath done great things for them.
> The Lord hath done great things for us;
> whereof we are glad.
>
> Psalm 126:1–3 (AV)

Bible translators often ignore it, but it is clear – many people, with one mouth and one tongue, speaking the same words and singing the same song. Drawn together by "Yeshua" to fulfil their destiny and inherit, not just a piece of the Middle East, but a restored earth and heaven together with all the tribes redeemed by Jesus. How gracious, and how merciful God is.

One from two

Paul reminded the Gentile Christians in Ephesus about the time they were separate from Christ. They were excluded from citizenship in Israel and foreigners to the covenants of promise, lost and without hope. What better way to conclude the subject of Israel's destiny with his words written 2,000 years ago but entirely relevant to a new millennium:

> But now in Christ Jesus you who once were far away have been brought near through the blood of Christ. For he himself is our peace, who has made the two one and has destroyed the barrier, the dividing wall of hostility, by abolishing in his flesh the law with its commandments and regulations. His purpose was to create in

himself one new man out of the two, thus making peace, and in this
one body to reconcile both of them to God through the cross, by
which he put to death their hostility . . . Consequently, you are no
longer foreigners and aliens, but fellow citizens with God's people
and members of God's household . . .

(Ephesians 2:13–16 & 19)

CHAPTER 19

GOD'S AMAZING TECHNICOLOURED DREAM CHURCH!

Visions of heaven

"I rose up out of my body and hovered, looking down at myself. Then I entered a dark tunnel and floated gently upwards. I had no idea of time. Suddenly, I burst out of the tunnel into a blaze of light and found myself in a beautiful garden. It was beyond description, unlike anything I had experienced. The colours of the flowers were iridescent, shining as if possessing a light of their own. The leaves of the trees shimmered like finest silk in shades incomparable with anything in this world.

The path between the trees was transparent gold; the sky was a thousand rainbows merging in a mist; it was difficult to tell where sky ended and grassy slopes began. The air, heavy with perfume, intoxicated me with its aroma. This fantastic display of colour was not garish, everything blended perfectly, the place exuded peace. Then I saw a man dressed in pure white, a band of glittering gold around his breast . . ."

This is a typical description from scores of people who claim to have died and visited "heaven," only to be sent back for some reason. The traumas and shakings which come our way provide windows of opportunity for good, or evil, to come into our lives. The heavenly world appears to be waiting to see our responses which either give access to God or to the enemy.

From one world to another

Every tremor, every shattering experience, can be a step into the presence of God or a slippery slope into bitterness and despair. Those who reach to Father escape into his arms and find comfort in the midst of trial. After a long period of illness and suffering, my own father lifted his head, looked beyond the darkened room where he lay and said, "I am entering a new and happy relationship!" Then he was gone.

I mentioned the *Divine Conspiracy* earlier. On the subject of death Dallas Willard says:

> Another picture is of one who walks to a doorway between rooms. While still interacting with those in the room she is leaving, she begins to see and converse with people in the room beyond, who may be totally concealed from those left behind. Before the use of widespread heavy sedation, it was quite common for those keeping watch to observe something like this.

We have no means of verifying stories of visiting heaven, although we cannot deny the sincerity often backed by a changed life. The Bible is not unsupportive. Paul speaks of "out of body" experiences, and someone he knew, perhaps himself, visited the "third heaven," (2 Corinthians 12:2). Ezekiel had great difficulty describing what took place "when the heavens opened and I saw visions of God." He could find no words to share what passed before his eyes. His frustration was obvious; he could only repeat such phrases as "what looked like" or "had the appearance of" or to combine the two for a change, "the appearance of the likeness of."

John in The Book of Revelation was also overwhelmed by the awesome majesty of what he saw. Seas of glass, streets of gold, walls of precious stones and gates of pearl and thousands upon thousands of worshippers blown away by the immensity of what they beheld. God is incredible – there's no end to his originality and artistry.

Monochrome church

How is it that so much of what we Christians do is monochrome and monotonous, when our God is so colourful and creative? How can we claim to represent him when we don't display his ingenuity? His children, made in his image, should act as he does. Maybe we had the creative stuffing knocked out of us when we joined the church?

Evangelicalism seems to breed fear that anything beautiful, enjoyable or costly will lead to temptation and sin. This paranoia stems from a negative reaction to a period in the church's history when art was worshipped and money was no object when it came to buildings and finery. Alongside this indulgence was the attitude that we will always have the poor with us, so let them remain poor.

Restoring the arts

Nevertheless, the old adage remains true, "the answer to abuse is not disuse but proper use." No revival will fulfill its purpose unless, among all else, the arts are restored to their rightful place. We desperately need "shaking" to loose us from fears and wrong attitudes, to come to terms with our identity as sons of God and release his creative Spirit among us. We must respect different skills, abilities and burdens the Lord has placed within us as individuals and encourage their function. No striving, demanding, or prima donna behaviour, but a recognition we all have a part to play in God's great plan and a duty to help one another find our place in the community.

Christine and I were listening to a couple share their sadness at failed attempts to build church and fulfill a leadership role for most of their Christian lives. It was an obvious case of "square peg in round hole." Knowing that Dinah's training was in fine arts and having seen her work, Christine exclaimed, "For heaven's sake, stop trying to be a church leader and start painting."

They took our advice and found a studio in Cyprus where Nigel, Dinah's husband, had once practised as a doctor. Laying aside fears it was too late in life, Dinah took up the brush with enthusiasm and Nigel gave her every support. Years on in her mid-seventies, Dinah Kendall is one of the country's leading religious artists. Her work is sought after, fetching thousands of pounds. It is the subject of articles and books, with invitations for exhibitions from prisons to cathedrals. Her work is making statements in places where no spoken ministry would ever be welcome.

Lucy Doran – pioneer

I was visiting South Africa with Gerald Coates and Noel Richards when we called on the Hatfield Christian Church in Pretoria. The leader, Francois Van Nierkerk, pointed us to an art exhibition they had laid on. Gerald and I shared some reluctance to look round, since not all our experiences of the mix of art and Christians could be described as "blessed." Noel, a philistine when it comes to art, according to Gerald, was not at all interested. Gerald knew he would have to visit the exhibition and prayed, "Dear Lord, please let there be one picture I like."

Finally, I went to the floor where the paintings were displayed.

I guessed that Lucy Doran, the artist who had put the exhibition together, would not be there and I would not have to make those non-committal "mmm's and ahhh's," such as we do after an unimpressive prophetic word. I was wrong; she was there. This was her baby and she didn't want to miss a trick.

As I walked round my jaw fell. This was something else. None of those splodgy abstracts with orange crosses leaping out of muddy backgrounds or doves that look like overweight seagulls, and there wasn't an angel in sight! What I saw was a brilliant array of original oils, watercolours and acrylics which took my breath away. I decided on two I wanted and went to find Gerald, who was looking for paintings to grace Waverley Abbey House in Surrey. His face was a mixture of amazement and relief and Lucy looked as if she'd won the lottery. "I'll have that one, that one, that one too – oh, yes and that one there and . . ." The pictures I'd chosen were gone before I could muster "But Gerald . . ."

Later I shared my vision for the arts with Lucy, "Creativity is what God is all about, we're made in his image. Leaders, preoccupied with the five m's – meetings, music, ministry, miracles and money, have neglected movement, colour, taste, smell and touch. We must use all means to celebrate and communicate the love God has for people and the joys and pains we experience in our struggle to know him."

"We've despised the arts and marginalized the artist," I continued, "and our churches do the same. There are few pastors who understand and can bridge the gap between local church and bruised and battered artists. Sadly, they don't fit our inflexible structures, but are best placed to influence whole sections of society otherwise unreached." Her eyes filled with tears, which told something of the journey Lucy Doran had come in her attempts to fulfill the calling God placed upon her.

Business on a mission

It's not only the arts that are pushed to the edges of church or outlawed as un-spiritual. We will only see beauty and colour restored when every skill co-operates to serve and glorify God. For example, business entrepreneurs are key to the development of all God wants us to do in society and mission. They will not only demonstrate biblical principles by bringing kingdom values to management and the marketplace, but they will also help create a new kind of missionary force.

The new breed of apostle we have been speaking of will not depend on charity alone, living in a protected cultural bubble in nations they serve. Their teams will contribute to the enhancement of those nations by providing work and investment as well as spiritual care – God's way is holistic.

Tragically business people and others have the impression they're second-class citizens, and to be truly, deeply spiritual they should be in "full-time" church-based ministry. Every Christian is "full-time" for God, each in different areas of calling and expertise pulling together to change the world. We have done wrong to draw these people into the structures of the church, causing pressure and frustration.

Rather than draw them in we should thrust them out, providing them, our professional people and all involved in society, with pastoral care, prayer backing, strategy and resources. Then they'll be effective as church ambassadors and missionaries. Dr Martin Robinson, director of mission and theology at the Bible Society in the UK, discovered in research that no revival changes the heart of a nation, nor do we see explosive growth, until Christians take kingdom values into key areas of life and work. Preaching and praying alone don't do it! We must empower those working at the coal face by giving them support and tools to reach their sphere with the gospel.

Using the altars to the unknown god

There is nowhere the Holy Spirit is not at work. Like Paul in Athens, we need to find the altar to the unknown god (Acts 17:23) which opens up a way to dialogue and discussion with those outside the circle of our experience. John Drane, Professor of Practical Theology at Aberdeen University and Professor of Evangelism at Fuller Theological Seminary, was in Australia visiting a theological college. There was a major New Age festival in town at the same time. John determined, with the support of the principal, to prayerfully visit the festival to discover the "altar" which would enable them to reach those needy people who were on a spiritual journey. Within five minutes he had found what he was looking for – Tarot cards!

In 1922 Arthur Waite designed the original 78 Tarot cards. There are other versions but these can be used, without compromise, to tell the Bible story. The imagery, symbolism and design is almost totally drawn from scripture. John is currently producing a book that explains this specially for New Agers. He and his colleagues returned to the festival in a booth, offering to "explain the true meaning of the Tarot." People piled in and the short story is that numbers were converted and some trained for the ministry at the college.

Furthermore, John's wife Olive was clearly led by the Lord, after the death of a child, to take up clowning. Later she was speaking to a large group using her role as a clown to introduce the gospel. Whilst talking she was putting on her clown clothes and make-up. The final thing was to apply the crosses to her eyes. At this point she asked if people would like to have the crosses painted on their eyes so they could see God's perspectives through the cross of Jesus.

Hundreds came forward, and there was a great deal of emotion as her team helped. Afterwards the phone didn't stop ringing. "What happens when we wash the crosses off? Will we stop seeing from God's perspective?" were the questions. The next day they returned to explain how people could continue to see through the cross. Many were saved and there is now a thriving church among those people.

In their book, *The Discovery of Genesis* (Concordia 1979) C.H. Kang and Ethel R. Nelson uncover scriptural links in the pictographs of early oriental languages. For example, the character or ideogram for "boat" is vessel + eight + person, clearly picturing the flood. The ideogram for "first" is life + dust + man, and "covet" is made from women + two trees and so on. Here are endless opportunities to introduce the Bible to those who share this language. On the other hand, the Japanese love comics, devouring billions every year. One Christian publisher is set to market comics which share exciting testimonies and thrilling Bible stories. The Lord will help us find keys to open the hearts of many peoples who have been closed for centuries.

Rediscovering the power of symbols

Our friends in historic churches will enjoy a wry smile as some in new churches rediscover the importance of symbols. During one of my first trips to India, teaching among tribal groups who had no written language and therefore no Bible, I realized the value of pictures and visual aids which is, no doubt, how icons originated. Thousands carrying torches on a march or using light-sticks to express witness in a stadium, is a powerful symbolism the Holy Spirit can use. Ribbons, banners or flags can immediately change the mood of worship with colour. Gold or orange may lift us into high praise, or pastel shades of blue or green into reflection and prayer.

Andy Au, a church leader who also moves prophetically, once brought our leaders' conference to its knees in tears. He danced during communion using red and white ribbons, speaking powerfully of cleansing blood and holiness. The ribbons seemed to fly up to heaven honouring Jesus, then fell gently around the shoulders of those kneeling in prayer. When he'd finished, the ribbons were used by David Matthews, one of our team at the time, to drape around people seeking God or carrying some pain. As we prayed, and the ribbons touched, many experienced immediate release. It was a special time that will long be remembered.

In the prayer gatherings at the church I attend, we sometimes use a long piece of blue material we call "the river." In 1998 Gerald Coates, founder of the church, began to take "the river" to conferences in different parts of the world. After preaching, he invited people to walk through or to just stand in "the river." We have witnessed amazing scenes as scores have met with God, experiencing conviction, healing, restoration and the evident presence of Jesus.

More recently, Stuart Lindsell, another ministry, prophesied that "the river" should go into the marketplace. Now we have seen non-Christians in shopping centres being bold enough to step into this symbol of God's power and peace for prayer. People are more open to God than we realize. Let us use God-given ingenuity to find ways to connect.

Redundant ministries

Few of us in "ministry" realize there will be no place for much of what we do in the kingdom. There will be no healing lines, no queues of people hoping that this time our touch, (or maybe push?) will be the one which brings wholeness – there will be no sick! No one will be wanting those mighty prophetic words we bellow forth in, not very accurate, 1611 King James English – prophecy will be fulfilled! There will be no adoring faithful to hang on our words as we share our revelation from Hezekiah 12:3 or Expectations 64:5 – they will know as much as we do!

I have a picture of downtown New Jerusalem where redundant prophets, teachers and healers sit on the sidewalk huddled in groups. Blankets round shoulders, an enamel mug or old cap laid on the ground with a sign (painted lovingly by an artist, canvas courtesy of a business person) – "spare a tithe – unemployed healing evangelist – skills no longer required!"

For many leaders ministry is an end in itself, rather than a means to an end. Their fulfilment is wrapped up in the ministry and they are dependent on people needing them. This leadership will not provide an atmosphere where others can find their place and flourish. Godly leadership will, of course, need to be resourced and served in order to achieve its kingdom objectives, but the end result will be people empowered, released and supported in their God-given calling too.

Let me draw on that wise old bird, Tom Marshall, again. He asked the question, "How powerful is the leader of a church of two hundred people where he, or she, has all the power?" He followed it with another; "How powerful is a leader of a church of two hundred where every individual is empowered?" There was no need to answer.

Crowned with glory and honour

We must provide an environment where everyone can find their reason for being. We will be amazed to discover what lies beneath the surface of even the most unlikely people, when the Holy Spirit is free to work through them. You see, the battle is for the soul. The human soul, touched by the Spirit of God, is the most powerful and creative thing in the universe outside of God himself. There is nothing else like it.

In Psalm 8 translators had difficulty coming to terms with

what's being said. David cries in amazement to God, ". . . What is man that you are mindful of him, the son of man that you care for him?" Then most versions go on, "You made him a little lower than the angels," or perhaps, "heavenly beings." This avoids the truth for scripture really says, God has made us a little lower than *himself*!

This makes more sense when we read on, "(You) crowned him with glory and honour. You made him ruler over the works of your hands; you put *everything* under his feet" (my italics). How can we expect to rule angels, as we're told we will elsewhere in scripture, if we are lesser beings (1 Corinthians 6:3)? No, alive in the Spirit, we possess divine nature (2 Peter 1:4), and are given "all authority in heaven and on earth" (Matthew 28:18).

Is it any wonder Satan wants us locked in prisons of self-doubt, legalism, control and division? This generation must break out and get their feet on his neck, claiming their inheritance in Jesus. Too long our enemy has been allowed to hold a monopoly in education, the arts, media, business, politics and the law. It is time to see his demise, not through arrogance and grasping, but by following Jesus' example. He quietly and confidently stood his ground, willing to pay for freedom with his life.

Technicoloured church

What a release this will bring to the church as the pure white light of God hits the prisms of our unfettered lives and splits into myriad brilliant coloured rainbow beams. The holiness and creativity of God will shine through his body, reflecting Jesus into every dark corner of the world. Each individual, family and culture bringing their treasures to lay at Jesus' feet.

The dancers, film-makers, potters, weavers, poets, architects, builders, jewellers, administrators, cooks, teachers, initiators, servants and many, many more bringing their skills to restore and beautify the living temple of our living God, in a fitting tribute to the one who bled and died to make this new technicoloured age of grace, creativity and everlasting joy a reality.

Hear Paul's words from his letter to the Ephesians encouraging them to appreciate God's intention for the church:

> I pray also that the eyes of your heart may be enlightened in order that you may know the hope to which he has called you, the riches of his glorious inheritance in the saints, and his incomparably great power for us who believe (1:18–19).
>
> And God placed all things under his [Jesus'] feet and appointed him to be head over everything for the church, which is his body, the fulness of him who fills everything in every way (1:22–23).
>
> In order that in the coming ages he might show the incomparable riches of his grace, expressed in kindness to us in Christ Jesus (2:7).
>
> For we are God's workmanship, created in Christ Jesus to do good works, which God prepared in advance for us to do (2:10).
>
> His intent was that now, through the church, the manifold [rainbow-coloured] wisdom of God should be made known . . . (3:10).
>
> . . . that you may be filled to the measure of all the fulness of God (3:19).
>
> . . . to him be glory in the church and in Christ Jesus throughout all generations, for ever and ever! Amen (3:21).

CHAPTER 20

STOP THE DAMNED DIVISION!

"The Sacrament of Unity and Love" Saint Fulgentius of Ruspe

'We who are many are one body, since we all share the same bread.' And so we pray that, by the same grace which made the Church Christ's body, all its members may remain firm in the unity of that body through the enduring bond of love.

We are right to pray that this may be brought about in us through the gift of the one Spirit of the Father and the Son. The holy Trinity, the one true God, is of its nature unity, equality and love, and by one divine activity sanctifies its adopted sons. That is why Scripture says that God's love has been poured into our hearts by the Holy Spirit he has given us. The Holy Spirit, who is the one Spirit of the Father and the Son, produces in those to whom he gives the grace of divine adoption the same effect as he received among those whom the Acts of the Apostles describes as having received the Holy Spirit. We are told that the company of those who believed were of one heart and soul, because the one Spirit of the Father and the Son, who with the Father and the Son is one God, had created a single heart and soul in all those who believed.

This is why Saint Paul in his exhortation to the Ephesians says that this spiritual unity in the bond of peace must be carefully preserved. "I, therefore, a prisoner for the Lord," he writes, "beg you to lead a

life worthy of your calling, with all humility and meekness and with patience, bearing with one another in love, eager to maintain the unity of the Spirit in the bond of peace. There is one body and one Spirit.'"
(From a book addressed to Monimus, Lenten/Easter Breviary II, Page 652)

Crippling division

Division among Christians is the single biggest hindrance to the church completing her mission to reach all peoples with the good news. This corporate objective, lovingly but firmly laid on us by Jesus is achievable in one generation if we co-operate. Jesus said, ". . . every city or household divided against itself will not stand" (Matthew. 12:25). Who says he was wrong?

One of the great divides in the church's development in England was between Celtic and Roman Christians. Chris Seaton describes this in *New Celts* written with Roger Ellis (Kingsway). It's my conviction that the Roman emphasis on order and maintenance combined with the Celtic emphasis on freedom and mission could have seriously affected this nation for good. Chris comments on this:

The possibility of the Celtic and Roman wells working for the same goals offers an awesome prospect in hindsight. The strengths of the Eastern and Western expressions of church could both have been expressed in these Islands. Order and energy, discipline and wandering, structure and freedom hand in hand would have been a dynamic mix.

Similarly, I wonder what might have happened had Wesley and Whitfield been fully united in their efforts to evangelize these islands. Would the combination of their gifts and understanding have produced a living stream that could have gone on to even greater things? Neither the Celts nor Whitfield left behind a continuing expression of their ministry, whereas the Romans and Wesley left structures with mixed blessings, but at least there's something to restore!

Apart from a few sacrificial saints over the centuries, the church would have failed with its history of infighting. Division, or conflicting vision, ultimately destroys any house which allows it to continue. The body of Christ is no exception; if the members are at war it is impossible for Jesus, the head, to co-ordinate his body. However, unity is not something we want in order to succeed. Unity is the outcome and evidence of a right response to Jesus. It is fundamental to our life in God and is of value in itself. Jesus is worthy of our expressions of it.

Amazing facts

After one hundred years of Christianity the ratio of non-Christians to Christians worldwide was approximately 360 to 1. By the end of the first millennium it had dropped to around 220 to 1 and by 1990 it had reached a staggering 7 to 1! And we're not talking nominal Christians – if that were the case it would be almost 3 to 1.

These amazing statistics are down to the power of our message and the determination of small sections of the church, many who died as martyrs. In fact, there were more Christian martyrs in the last century alone, than in the rest of the church's history. As I write, the church in some countries is suffering massive persecution and wholesale slaughter. Strangely, these are often the areas of the greatest growth.

Concerning the unreached, in AD 100 there was just one church for every 12 unreached groups. Each church would have had to send 12 missionaries for each unreached group to have one worker. Today there are 600 churches for every unreached group, and we would only need to increase giving by 0.01% to resource the 48,000 missionaries needed to send four workers to each unreached people!

These statistics do not account for the huge growth among Charismatics and Pentecostals, by far the fastest growing movement in the worldwide church. In 1900 there were no more than four million, whereas today there are over 500 million. In other words, almost 10% of the world's population has experienced a powerful baptism in the Holy Spirit! The task of world mission is well within our reach, if we focus on the central issues which unite us.

Unity of Spirit

Why is it, with this tremendous potential, we allow the enemy to divert us? Poised on the edge of our greatest opportunity in 2,000 years Satan convinces us that unity of doctrine is more important than unity of Spirit, when it's exactly the opposite.

Paul pleads with the Ephesians, "Make every effort to keep the unity of the Spirit through the bond of peace" (4:3) . . . "until we all reach unity in the faith and in the knowledge of the Son of God and become mature" (4:13). Unity of Spirit is a gift, to be maintained. You cannot maintain what you do not possess. Unity of faith is a process we are called to work towards. Why do sound Bible-believing Christians twist and mangle scripture? They did it over the baptism in the Spirit, the nature of church, and now they tell us that a common understanding of truth comes before a common experience of the Holy Spirit, when we need the Spirit to lead us into truth!

So how does unity come?

I'm not suggesting we compromise for unity, simply that we approach one another with kindness and generosity, believing the best and affirming the life of Jesus wherever we see it. By all means debate, but with forbearance and patience, giving way to one another and listening carefully without a critical or cynical spirit. We'll discover that kernels of truth can be hidden by the husks of immaturity.

Let me repeat, unity is a gift of the Spirit. Paul assures us ". . . we were all baptized by one Spirit into one body" (1 Corinthians 12:13). At the outset we are bound together in Christ. "Unity of the Spirit" comes by faith; we then work tirelessly to keep it through patience, honesty and tolerance. In such an atmosphere we grow and develop, learning to love and trust one another. We become interdependent, aware that every individual or group has a contribution to our corporate life and wellbeing. If, alongside this openness and willingness to listen, we release intercessors and peacemakers we will have a powerful recipe for healing and reconciliation.

Truth and counter truth

Each tradition and movement has its distinctive features and emphases which help us know Jesus better. Polarization and division cause "characteristics" to become "caricatures" as we exaggerate truth to counter opposition. Exaggerated truth means those who see the other end of God's large spectrum of truth cannot relate to us.

Every truth has counter truth which seems in conflict, but in Christ is reconciled. Mercy and judgement, or faith and works, like the wings of a bird, work in harmony for flight to take place. A wing has beauty in itself and is aerodynamic, but thrown into the air it will fall to the ground. Worse, a bird with only one wing may be very much alive, and have great beauty, but it will never fly.

The church is full of opinionated people and evangelicals are the worst, because we claim scripture supports our views. The problem with scripture is that truth is hidden like precious stones or metal waiting to be mined. The key to the discovery of truth is firstly to do with humility and secondly with relationships. We are plainly told God reveals himself to the humble (Matthew 11:25), and scripture is not for private interpretation (2 Peter 1:20 AV).

Jesus also warned us that he spoke in parables so we wouldn't understand, whereas we feel that parables make truth obvious. We have lost the art of seeking and the sense of mystery. Truth is reduced to "systematic theology" which can be learned and assimilated. Accuracy takes precedence over heart and practice. As Jesus pointed out there is such a thing as being dead right with emphasis on *dead* (Matthew 23: 2–4).

Truth is a person . . .

Jesus spoke about these people when he said, ". . . do everything they tell you. But do not do what they do, for they do not practise what they preach" (Matthew 23:3). So, our talk may be true, but if it is not spoken in the Spirit of Jesus, backed by godly practice, it's not "the truth." Truth is more than words, truth is a person incarnate in Jesus.

Truth must be translated into lifestyle and mixed with grace. Truth without grace is destructive, grace without truth is sentiment. So we need one another to represent Jesus and be salt and light in the world. Like the ordinary people who received Jesus and his teaching with delight (Mark12:37), many are waiting for a fresh breeze of living truth, perfumed with the fragrance of love, to blow from the church which, historically, has caused so much pain.

... who sees with different eyes

As the scribes and Pharisees of Jesus' day saw the speck in their brother's eye and ignored the plank in their own, we can do the same. Being proud of our rightness and failing to see goodness in others is self-righteousness, and God hates this intensely. The Lord can cope with a broken sinner, but a proud Christian is no fun to be with.

A godly preacher found himself in a railway carriage with a drunk. The drunk was talkative and generous with his bottle, and continually offered it to the man of God, who politely declined. After many refusals the drunkard, full of remorse, said, "You must think I'm a terrible sinner?" "Not at all," the preacher replied, "I was thinking how generous you are with something so precious to you!"

The stronger brother

If only we adopted this attitude. Not that we ignore sin, but our first thought is to see good in one another rather than misreading motives, mishearing words and misjudging intentions. One day the Lord will replay the video tapes, and we'll be embarrassed to see how petty, obnoxious and how wrong we were in many situations.

Often, in an attempt to excuse this awful critical and judgmental behaviour, we label that kind of person "the weaker brother or sister". Perhaps they malign someone for drinking a glass of wine, for wearing certain clothes or holding a different view. Such a person is not the "weaker brother," he is the "stronger brother" and should be disciplined for his dominant, controlling spirit. "Oh, but we may offend him," or "even lose him" I hear. Sadly, these people need to be offended and our churches might be better off without them. They're usually the reason why others, who are really seeking God and struggling to understand him, do not come.

Gerald Coates was preaching in a small church on law and grace. He was underlining God's kindness and how he viewed legalistic Bible reading and quiet-times. Suddenly a man jumped up shouting, "These young people should be up early in the morning seeking God!" Gerald was taken aback and for once lost for words. The man's wife came to Gerald's aid. "If that's what you believe," she said to her husband, "why don't *you* do it then?" Be sure hypocrisy will find you out.

How to disagree . . .

Disagreements are not disaster, they are an integral part of life, but we must learn how to disagree, how to be angry without sinning (Ephesians 4:26). Disagreement is not sin, and anger is not necessarily sin. It is how we disagree and how we express emotion which is important. Christine used to say I was "nicer than God" and outside the family, I had a "ministry of hinting." Preach a sermon on giving and the generous will give more, but the mean will remain mean. There's nothing like being direct. I would approach people who needed discipline, apart from Christine and the children, with a super-spiritual pleasantness which meant they never heard what I was saying.

One day I read "be ye angry, and sin not" (Ephesians 4:26 AV) and determined to be more honest. One brother, a long-term nuisance, came to see me with his gripes. I let him have it straight, and tears filled his eyes. "What have I done?" I thought, ready to apologize and revert to niceness. "Now I know you care," he wept. "You're only honest like this with people you love. Now I feel one of the family." I'd made a friend for life.

Where there is unresolved conflict it should be natural to

address it in the context of relationships in the family, among friends or in the church. Mutual submission is a scriptural principle and provides the means to deal with differences where there's love and respect. Even in the world, we must accept the judgement of peers if we're called to account! How much more should we, in the church, find loving and honest ways to solve our problems?

... and how to divide

Even division is not sin if done in the right way. Our hero Abraham explained to his cousin Lot that, because they were brothers, and in order to avoid strife between their camps, it would be better to separate (Genesis 13:7–12). But Abraham's heart was for Lot and the moment his relative was in difficulty he was there to help, risking all to save him (14:12–16). Most of us wait until things are so bad we drive one another away by the pain we cause, and then there's little hope of reconciliation.

The prodigal's father knew how to release his son. The boy was wrong but dad kept the cord of love intact, letting it out so, at the right time, he could pull it in again. In our disagreements we play what I call the "conscience card" too soon. We use conscience to blackmail one another. Obviously, we must obey God and our conscience, but mostly we are too easily offended and our consciences are too tender. If we were God we'd have no friends. Friendship requires love, tolerance and patience.

Rediscovering the true pastors

Part of the answer to division is the restoration of the pastoral ministry of Ephesians 4. Let me explain. Just as someone who prophesies is not necessarily a prophet, or someone who sings a singer, neither is someone who shows care necessarily a pastor. The gift embraces leadership as well as function and contains qualities like love, discipline, empowerment, care and feeding. We have different perceptions of "the pastor." For some a pastor leads, for others a pastor is a counsellor, someone who cares. The image varies from a leader to one who shows concern.

These models perpetuate wrong thinking and are unhelpful. I've said the words in scripture for pastor, elder, shepherd, overseer and bishop are interchangeable, but the word which most vividly describes the ministry in the English language and most powerfully expresses its function, is "shepherd."

When Jesus was born there were shepherds (plural) abiding together in the fields. They were together in the fields watching out for one another and their flocks. That's what pastors do. In a given location the pastors, in relationship, watch out for each other and the flocks of the one flock of God. The imagery of the shepherd runs through both Testaments and study shows us how the ministry functions.

Shepherds are responsible for the welfare of the whole flock, not just a part. They are firm not sentimental, hence the rod. They are concerned for the protection of all and will risk life and limb to ensure it. Often, pastors today care more about their position than working for the good of all. They want to be in control.

This model of a leadership has been described as "Snow White and the seven dwarfs!" The pastor is a "beautiful" person who surrounds himself with little people who are no threat. As we yield our leadership to God, he will raise up shepherds with peacemaking ministry who will work together to heal our divisions. These women and men, Christ's gifts to the body, will "equip the saints for the work of ministry," so that the church becomes the "shepherd" in the community at large.

Head of a mouse?

It has been prophesied, "The day of the streams is over, the day of the river is here!" This is true, but we must play our part to make it a reality. My Irish friend David Matthews, when referring to divisions among Protestants in Northern Ireland, said, "They'd rather be the head of a mouse than the tail of a lion!" If God's heart for unity is to be satisfied, we must give up our independence and need to control.

In coming together we provide a context where people can flourish and grow. Referring to the chart at the end of chapter 7, if the first reformation restored the "power of the word," the second restored the "power of the ministry," and the third restored the "power of the Spirit" then this present reformation will restore the "power of the people." How will this happen?

For years now I have been involved in charismatic renewal. It has been thrilling and a privilege. However, the emphasis has been typically Protestant – the baptism of the individual Christian in the Holy Spirit. Here, my *personal experience* of the Spirit is added to my *personal salvation* and helps me find my *personal calling*, which gives me *personal fulfilment*. This is not totally unscriptural but it is not scriptural either. The biblical teaching concerning our destiny as individuals is related to, and dependent upon, the rest of the people of God. We have no future outside of our relationship in the community of the redeemed.

Tail of a lion!

Over and over in the Acts it is recorded that the Holy Spirit fell on gathered saints. This corporate baptism is in tune with the historical picture of a gathered people coming out from the bondage of Egypt and through baptism in the Red Sea together, before entering the land of promise. John's assurance, "he will baptize you with the Holy Spirit and with fire" would have been understood by his Jewish hearers as personal and corporate. Emmanuel means "God with us," not "God with me." We journey together; we are baptized into common joys, sufferings and hopes as one people. If I must be the tail of the lion to enjoy this, so be it.

This understanding comes with baptism by the Spirit into the body (1 Corinthians 12:13) and frees us from independence which focuses on "my" needs and ministry. Without this mindset, which has dogged the church for centuries, we become a Spirit-led people, recognizing all the gifts Christ has placed within the body.

The impartation of this common anointing is an essential part of what God is doing in the church now, and we should pray for the Spirit to come in this way. After such blessing, those early Christians were of one heart and one soul, an unforgettable encounter which blew away their fears. Jesus had commanded his disciples to wait together in one place. In that upper room the Spirit came and the whole company received the blessing – same place, same time. Together they became powerful witnesses to the historic events surrounding Jesus' life and to the coming kingdom.

No competition

In June 1999 I was privileged to work in a team with Martin Scott's "Sowing Seeds For Revival" in the Erewash Valley, the East Midlands of England. It was Robin Hood country, but hardly the centre of the universe! The ministry encourages reconciliation, prayer and co-operation among leaders in key areas. For some years, a group of leaders had prayed together for revival: an Assemblies of God and an Elim pastor, an Anglican vicar, a Baptist pastor and the leader of a Church of the Nazarene. At the start there had been suspicion and jealousy, even to the point of avoiding one another in the street.

As they prayed, every morning at 6:30am, the barriers came down. God gave them real love for one another, and now they long to see each other's churches prospering even at their own expense. Every church in the valley, regardless of denomination, was repeatedly visited and prayed over. The spiritual temperature is rising in those depressed mining communities and since our week with them more leaders, including a Methodist minister, have joined to pray.

Competition has been an issue for many church leaders. The second question we ask when we meet after "which church?" is "how many members?" But competition is biblical, Hebrews 10:24 speaks of provoking "unto love and to good works" (AV) and I recall another version calls us to "outdo one another in love!"

A sevenfold strategy to help us reach our goals

If we're to achieve our objectives of co-operation, there are things we must prayerfully keep in mind, and use as a checklist to see how we're progressing. You could call it a sevenfold strategy to help us reach our goal of unity:

1. *Respect identity* – if you are secure in yourself, you will not pressure others to conform to your ways. You will respect their right to find God for themselves and develop their distinctives as individuals, or as a group. Diversity will be encouraged and welcomed.
2. *Develop relationships* – find time to nurture friendships which go beyond the necessary business of function. Eating

and drinking with friends was an essential part of Jesus' life and should be a regular feature of our relationships too, along with walking, chatting and enjoying simple things together.

3. *Listen to one another* – dialogue and debate are vital in the process of understanding one another's burdens and concerns, but listening is essential for real and abiding harmony. Richard Dobbins, director of Emerge Ministries in Akron, Ohio, warns married couples, "don't shoot from the lip! Careless words can cost you hours of painful attempts to explain what you meant – sometimes in the middle of the night!" We leaders do well to heed his wisdom.

What we say in the heat of the moment is rarely what we mean. We must allow one another to retract things. James 1:19 should be read before we get down to the serious business of sorting issues, "My dear brothers, take note of this: Everyone should be quick to listen, slow to speak and slow to become angry . . ."

4. *Serve one another* – break the hierarchies and pecking orders of our structures and find ways to humbly serve. Be sensitive to one another's physical and emotional needs, take time out to show kindness and tenderness. If our master humbled himself to wash his disciples' feet, how much more should we bless and encourage each other.

5. *Invest outside your own sphere* – offering practical help and sharing resources, particularly finances, is a wonderful way of dispelling suspicion and fear. I recently heard of a church in the USA which took an offering for another struggling church's building fund. They closed down their Sunday meeting and popped across to take the gift as a surprise. We will not be truly blessed until we invest in others outside our circle of relationships.

6. *Recognize and receive from others* – in the West we tend

towards paternalism, "I help you, you don't help me," and Christians are worst in this respect. This leads to pride and insensitivity on the one hand, and loss of dignity and wrong dependence on the other. If we are all God's children is it possible that some of us have nothing to share? We must learn to receive from others. We will be amazed at the jewels God has placed in the lives of those different from us.

7. *Take time to network* – in-breeding produces over-bred creatures with exaggerate features, weak and prone to disease. Cross-fertilization keeps a strain strong and healthy. Love for the body of Christ will compel us to network across cultures sub-cultures, people groups, nations, generations and denominations. Only a fool neglects part of his own body. Every member brings their special contribution.

Our divisions work against a corporate baptism in the Spirit and God will hold us responsible, particularly leaders. Unity draws down God's blessing like a magnet. So, let's stop this damned division and come together to wait patiently for the Spirit. He will come and bind our hearts and souls together in a heavenly baptism of love. Then, like those early saints, we'll be less concerned for ourselves and more concerned for the lost. Thus turned inside out we will, as one people, turn the world upside down!

Prophetic postscripts UK and USA

During October 1999 I was attending a regular forum in UK for apostolic team leaders. These men (sadly no women here) have known one another for years and, whilst each team has its distinctives, we have a great regard for one another and enjoy genuine friendship. Our sharing reflects this love and trust and is open and honest.

In the midst of reporting good things taking place, there was a concern that churches were not growing. The question was – have the New Churches plateaued? In the debate Derek Brown reminded us of a prophetic word attributed to the great pente-costal revivalist Smith Wigglesworth[1] just before he died in 1947. As he read it a shiver of excitement ran down my spine. Could this be the moment?

During the next few decades there will be two distinct moves of the Holy Spirit across the church in Great Britain. The first move will affect every church that is open to receive it and will be character-ized by a restoration of the baptism and gifts of the Holy Spirit. The second move of the Holy Spirit will result in people leaving his-toric churches and planting new churches.

In the duration of each of these moves, the people who are involved will say "This is the great revival". But the Lord says "No, neither is the great revival but both are steps towards it."

When the new church phase is on the wane, there will be evi-denced in the churches something that has not been seen before: a coming together of those with an emphasis on the Word and those with an emphasis on the Spirit. When the Word and the Spirit come together, there will be the biggest movement of the Holy Spirit that the nation, and indeed the world, has ever seen. It will mark the beginning of a revival that will eclipse anything that has been wit-nessed within these shores, even the Wesleyan and the Welsh revi-vals of former years. The outpouring of God's Spirit will flow over from the UK to the mainland of Europe, and from there will begin a missionary move to the ends of the earth.

Just prior to this word on 2 March 1946, Charles Price, one of the first North American healing evangelists, also prophesied before his death:

The greatest revival the world has ever seen is in preparation. Before it comes there will be a scourge of divine healers advertising their

wares and dogmas. They will speak of power in their bodies and
hands and of angelic visitations. The results will be the deifying of
man and this false move will precede the true revival and will
damage the children of God almost beyond repair.

Price's word implied a purging which would rid the church of
commercialism and greed and restore faith in the ministry as
integrity and the supernatural come together. This has been
happening in the USA in recent years. Now, with Toronto,
Pensacola and other centres of revival appearing it seems the
fires are beginning to burn.

My conviction is that "word and Spirit," or "holiness and
miracles" or "character and power," are the two witnesses
which God requires as heralds of his kingdom. In Revelation
11 and Zechariah 4 these "anointed ones," "sons of fresh oil,"
embody the spirit of "Moses" and "Elijah," the symbolic representatives of the law and the prophets. Fully visible in Jesus'
life and ministry, they are yet to be seen in fullness in his body.
However, Acts 1:8 confidently declares that we, God's people,
shall be his witnesses when the Holy Spirit comes upon us. The
church will, at some crucial point in history, become the
"Moses" and "Elijah" who display the character and power of
Jesus. Creation groans in anticipation of the day

This union of "word" and "Spirit" will not be a combination
of the worst elements of charismatic independence and desire
for personal fulfillment, with conservative evangelical legalism
and boring biblical lecturing. That would be a disaster of mon-
umental proportions and will never produce revival. In these
prophetic words, I hear God calling us to a new passion for
Jesus – the living word, revealed in scripture – the written word;
and to a new surrender to the Spirit who empowers. There's no
going back. The blessing of word and spirit will come as we
journey on together.

Notes

1. There are various reports of this prophecy and it is not clear exactly how, when or even whether Wigglesworth gave it in this form. However, the essential ingredients have been present since Wigglesworth's day. Clive Price's article in *Christianity*, May 2000, provides more information.

CHAPTER 21

THE WARFARE – TOGETHER WE STAND

The feel good factor

Spiritual warfare is currently a subject of great interest and controversy. The question, apart from the obvious – "Is our practice biblical?" is – "Has it been effective?" We may have prayed, fasted, shouted at the devil and feel very fulfilled, but has it made a scrap of difference? I believe in spiritual warfare, but we must judge effectiveness by results.

Business, industry and the professions are facing the challenge of performance-related measures, yet Christians hide behind well-worn, super-spiritual excuses – "eternity alone will reveal . . ." The truth is, "eternity *will* reveal:" it will reveal that much of our effort was born of the flesh, raised in pride and died in failure. Trouble is, some genuine saints who laboured and prayed, usually in secret and unknown, don't yet see the results of their warfare. Their names will go down as giants of intercession, but the rest of us must link our prayers to visible, tangible answers and measurable change or we'll lose credibility.

In the 1970s when spiritual warfare was rediscovered, the saints would sing and shout in conferences, wave their arms and stamp their feet for an hour or two and end up binding the demons over Britain. When the leaders felt they'd done enough, they'd all go back to their tents feeling better and have a nice cup of tea. Problem was, they'd end up shouting (quietly because of the family in the next tent), waving their arms at the wife and probably belting the kids because they'd played truant from the young people's meeting. All this showed the demon responsible for the campsite had escaped the effects of the national binding prayers.

Intercessors and apostolic leadership

This situation polarized the charismatic movement into "super-real" pragmatics and "so-heavenly-minded-no-earthly-use" intercessors. Things are changing. The intercessory movement is growing and maturing. There is a willingness for accountability and apostolic leaders are welcome to give oversight to the prayer movement. Respect between streams and a conviction concerning our need of one another will contribute to success.

Ed Delph, founder of N.A.T.I.O.N.s, "Networking Apostolic Thrust Internationally Or Nationally" in Phoenix, Arizona, was speaking at an intercessory conference in Westminster, London, England in May 1999. His message, entitled "Apostolic Intercession," underlined the importance of apostolic streams giving covering to the intercessory movement. This, he believes, will release power which will affect the highest echelons of society and government. He sees the link between the prayer networks and "tribal" leaders as a key to breakthrough in evangelism and bringing the bride of Christ to maturity.

At our Pioneer leaders conference in February 2000, five

South Africans from black and mixed-race churches made a deep and lasting impact by their presence, humility and contributions, which were powerful and moving. In private, Roger Petersen, pastor of Cape Town Christian Fellowship, prophesied that God longs for apostolic leaders and intercessors to work together to give oversight to the intercessors and keep them from enemy attacks provoked by their work. He warned that intercessors felt exposed, insufficiently supported and separated from leadership.

Later David Mniki, leader of Kholo Mission Centre in Idutywa, fasted and prayed for some days in my home. The Lord gave him a further revelation:

> The Lord was showing me something more about the prophetic responsibility of intercession, and the apostolic task of building. Although there is no exclusiveness implied, it is only in Christ that both functions were equally and adequately integrated. He could truly say that he could "*do* only what he sees the Father *do*" and claim "what I have *heard* from him I tell the world." But, in us, since the *doing* and the *hearing* are not normally centred in one person, it is essential that the *hearing* intercessors are closely linked to and listened to by the *doing* apostolic leaders.

24–7 prayer

At the same conference Pete Greig, a Pioneer leader, told us how the Lord had led him to start what has evolved into a worldwide prayer movement. It began after he visited the site of the hundred year prayer meeting which started in Hernnhutt on 13 August 1727. Pete was convinced the Lord wanted him to initiate a 24-hour 7 days a week prayer meeting for youth in his church, but couldn't believe that they'd cope, even for a short period. Not only did they cope but they carried on and became the inspiration for youth in churches round the globe. Their website is www.24-7prayer.com, and you'll find everything you need to get involved.

In the Roman Catholic Church too there is a return to emphasise prayer. Pope John Paul II wrote with regard to prayer:

Dear brother and sisters, our Christian communities must become genuine "schools" of prayer, where meeting with Christ is expressed not just in imploring help but also in thanksgiving, praise, adoration, contemplation, listening and ardent devotion, until the heart truly "falls in love."

Blessed Elena Guerra, founder of the Oblate Sisters of the Holy Spirit, is an inspiration to many prayer and intercession initiatives. Between 1895 and 1903 she wrote 12 letters to the Pope requesting renewed preaching on the Holy Spirit and prayer:

Pentecost is not over. In fact it is continually going on in every time and in every place, because the Holy Spirit desired to give himself to all men . . . we have only to dispose ourselves like them (first believers) to receive him well, and he will come to us as he did to them.

Oh, if only . . . unanimous and fervent prayers could be raised to Heaven in every part of Christendom, as they were once in the Cenacle (upper room) of Jerusalem for a rekindling of the Divine Spirit.

The trident . . .

As I have pondered this vital area of dealing with evil principalities and powers, I have concluded we must give the enemy a taste of his own medicine – the trident! We must hit him with the three-pronged fork on which, until now, he's had the monopoly. Using *heaven*, *earth* and *hell* as terms to describe the primary influences in our lives, that is i) God and his angels, ii) people and material things, iii) the devil and his demons, let's see how the Lord wants this threefold initiative in our hands.

Satan's been at work in the heavenly realm confusing communications between Christians and our commander Jesus. He has poured out unbelief and cynicism causing some to doubt his existence and the existence of a major source of help, the angels who faithfully serve God and watch over us. He has punished us on earth through infiltration with worldliness and direct persecution. Finally, he unleashed the forces of hell, disguised as angels of light, to corrupt, deceive and blind unsuspecting saints. The time's come to grasp the trident and turn it upon Satan himself!

... heaven, earth and hell

In every circumstance the three prongs of heaven, earth and hell bring their influences to bear. Hence our questions when trouble comes – was it God, was it man or was it the devil? Those questions were on everyone's lips when Diana, Princess of Wales tragically died on 31 August 1997. Did God intervene to stop a terrible mistake in the relationship with Dodi? Was it man, unscrupulous paparazzi, feeding a news-hungry public who demanded ever more titillating stories to placate their insatiable appetite for scandal? Or was it the devil who snuffed out this beautiful but strangely sad life in anger, for the good she was doing?

As always the answer was yes to all three. Heaven, earth and hell were all at work to turn the situation for good, for personal gain or evil. Remember Job from chapter six? Heaven, hell and earth were playing their parts in his experience. The Lord was deeply involved with his hidden agenda to bless; Satan, burning with hatred, longed to destroy God's faithful servant; and the three friends, motivated by self-justification and blinded by ignorance, were bending Job's ear to no effect.

Today the Lord calls his divided church to stand together using the kingdom authority at our disposal. He calls us to join forces to invade our time and this generation's space with the victory he secured; to exercise his authority over powers in *heavenly* realms, on *earth* and in *hell*. He's given us the power if we work together.

Charismatics, social activists and evangelicals

Charismatics emphasize spiritual warfare and direct their energies towards the *heavens*. They have sought to engage principalities who control the territories Satan put in their charge. Christian social activists confronted those same spirits on *earth* in the structures of society where greed and injustice rule. Through these channels Satan works his plan to bring humanity into subjection to himself. Evangelicals endeavoured to plunder hell and release captives through preaching a gospel true to scripture. Each, with the highest motives, has tried to serve God and be obedient to him. Each has tended to despise the other, believing their part is of primary importance. Such thinking must be abandoned it is misguided arrogance.

I have been amazed recently to see leading evangelicals, social activists and Charismatics humbly acknowledge their ineffectiveness and affirm their need of one another with tears. I have watched them kneel in repentance asking for prayer and forgiveness from those they have criticized. God will honour this, and every genuine movement we make towards unity. Let's use the trident to launch a simultaneous attack on the enemy through word, works and wonders which shake the foundations of hell, earth and heaven to put Satan in retreat.

The turning point in Revelation 12

In Revelation 12:1–11 the battle turns. The woman conceives. Her man-child, snatched from the jaws of the dragon, is caught up to the throne, God's seat of authority. Immediately there's war in heaven, the dragon is cast down to earth with his angels. "Now have come the salvation and the power and the kingdom of our God, and the authority of his Christ," the voice proclaims. The "accuser of our brothers" is on the run. How has this been achieved?

There are different schools of thought as to the symbolism of this passage. It has been argued the woman variously represents Eve, Mary, Israel and the church. The principle of a virgin conceiving and bringing forth a deliverer child is biblical, historic and ongoing. It is in the latter sense it is expressed here as Revelation opens with the promise we are to be shown "what must soon come to pass", in other words it is looking to a future fulfillment. You don't need revelation about what's already happened. So, the woman is primarily a picture of the church, Christ's body on the earth, destined to give birth to an overcoming company, indwelt by Jesus, sharing his authority.

That the "man-child" is a corporate group is clear from verse 11, where we are told "*They* [plural] overcame" (my italics). This would-be company of overcomers is suddenly "caught up" to the throne, preoccupied with God's authority. They are not swept away to a distant space safe-haven; they simply take the place reserved for them in this life and sit with Jesus in heavenly places (Ephesians 1:3/2:6). From this position of highest authority in heaven they visibly overpower the dragon and his angels on earth, through the victory already accomplished in hell by Jesus' death on the cross.

So the battle moves from heaven, to earth and finally to hell as Satan is "cast down" and exposed for what he really is.

Christ's salvation is revealed to break the bondage of demonic lies and accusations. This new generation of overcomers, born from the womb of the church, rediscover the truth Jesus modelled, that life and power are God's gifts to those who die to self. The cross remains the only route to the throne – "They overcame him by the blood of the Lamb and by the word of their testimony; they did not love their lives so much as to shrink from death" (v. 11).

The threefold cord

Our right in Christ places us in the throne room of *heaven* and once there, the challenge of *earth* and *hell* are already decided. But it is a corporate, overcoming company who initiate the beginning of the end. The three prongs of the trident, working in unison, finally dislodge the enemy. To change the analogy, in the words of Ecclesiastes "a threefold cord is not quickly broken" (4:12 AV).

The trident is a powerful weapon, and a "threefold cord" is extremely strong. A united effort by charismatics, social activists and evangelicals is what the Holy Spirit has been working for through renewal, restoration and revival. Personal renewal puts us in a right relationship to God – that's heaven in our hearts; church restoration put us in a right relationship to one another – that's glory on earth; and revival breaks demonic powers – that's hell open for prisoners to go free. Intercession, justice and proclamation working hand in hand will trigger God's final shakings in the heavens, on earth and in hell itself.

Surprise compliment

Pioneer People, the church I'm part of now, has been around for three decades. It has a wonderful history since it was planted by Gerald Coates. This church and, indeed, the whole Pioneer network[1] has been facing the challenge of implementing the change I'm writing about, and inevitably there is pain. Our self-image became tarnished, but the Lord is good! Into this turbulent period the Lord sent one of his angels, Brennan Manning, a Roman Catholic from the USA.

Brennan, author of *The Ragamuffin Gospel* (Multnomah Books USA), has a special way of introducing "Abba," "Daddy," our Father who was at the core of Jesus' relationship with heaven, and constantly upheld him through every test. It is obvious Brennan shares this intimate knowledge of the Father: it shines out. In his final address he encouraged us with these words which surprised many embroiled in the "important" and painful business of change:

> In the ten days I've spent here, you have treated me like Jesus. You have shown me such incredible hospitality, such a non-judgemental acceptance of a Roman Catholic, a sense of gentleness, such kindness. The signs of welcome that have abounded made me feel like I had known you for years, like I'm one of the Pioneer People. I can truthfully say I have been stunned by it. I have wept at night – that somebody would make a fuss over me. This is the only time in all my travels I have ever seen a Christ-centred, charismatic spirituality wedded to a deep concern for social justice, for social action, for Kosovo, for concern for the poor, I have been thrilled to see the whole gospel brought together, the love of God and the love of neighbour . . .
>
> The second thing that has struck me forcefully and humbled me, is the utter seriousness. I don't mean being solemn (there's a great deal of laughter in your community) but the seriousness about loving Jesus and following him, cost what it may. This has been such a life giving, such a rich experience for me . . . I ask the Lord to bless you . . .

It was a revelation, the "threefold cord" of word, works and wonders, was to some degree at least, woven into the fabric of our lives. If we can hold together in love and commitment, we will impact the territory God has entrusted to us.

Crisis and process

There are two ways of retrieving territory, by crisis or by process. Crisis removes the one in control, process takes the ground inch by inch. Both are recognized tactics of regular warfare. Whichever is successful, the other will need to be actioned to follow up. Take out the leader and those dominated by him must be made aware, even convinced, of the new situation. Take an area street by street and at some point the leader must be removed to secure the victory.

Process and crisis are equally important if we're to see towns, cities, regions, even nations cleared and released from oppressive influences of demonic powers. If, through fasting, intercession and challenging injustice, we break the demonic stronghold in an area, that's a major crisis victory. The effects should immediately be felt in a change of atmosphere and a new openness to the gospel. However, if we do not see that breakthrough, we should continue the process, taking ground little by little, household by household, street by street.

Putting my own life in order, I wrest the territory of my soul from the enemy's grip. If I do the same in my family, I claim more ground. Prayer walking my street and bringing reconciliation among neighbours is another step. Moving on to school or workplace broadens the claw-back and marginalizes ruling principalities. The more people who are involved in claiming ground like this, the greater the impact. In this way Wesleyan revival saved Britain from bloody revolution such as took place in France.

Can a nation be changed? Yes, nations can be changed by crisis or process but most effectively by the two working at every level: in *heaven*, on *earth* and in *hell*. Many in the UK look back on the 1960s as a dark time. Christians had been hoodwinked into believing that social action or involvement in politics was unspiritual. During those days many biblical foundations of government were undermined, and new legislation opened the door to the immorality, corruption and evil practices which abound today.

Moving the goalposts

Now we are more aware and a growing number of Christian agencies help monitor and lobby politicians, local governments and corporations. This is good news, but our enemy, master tactician as he is, has moved the goalposts. Whilst we tinker around with matters of national concern and internal interest, he has been at work infiltrating corridors of power in Europe and the UN. We are not now asleep, but we failed to notice that the game is being played on a different field.

Plans are in place for a new all-embracing super-religion which will marginalize "non-kosher" churches and Christian organizations. Dirk Paterson, Christian Solidarity World-Wide, exposes this in a paper, "Cults and the European Union – a reflection for UK Churches." What is planned will limit our activities as Christians, erode what remnants of family life remain and undermine our godly values.

We are beginning to experience the effects in Europe and the USA in discrimination against Christians. This is seen in education, what we're allowed to teach our children, sex education and restrictions on prayer; the matter of adoption – who is suitable; the use of buildings, noise in worship, proselytizing and who we are allowed to employ. There is also positive discrimination toward people of other faiths.

Thank God for those who are alerting us to what is going on. Pete Gardner with "Global Focus"[2] is one such lonely watchman prayer-walking the corridors of power in the UN and global governance forums. He is mobilizing Christians and is looking to lobby committees, advisory groups and organizations responsible for the development of future policy and international law. He also provides opportunities for prayer on site at key international events.

It may be too late. I believe the die is cast, and a global controller is inevitable. Nevertheless, we must sound the alarm and uncover the plot so people can choose who and what they'll serve. After all Joel prophesies: "Multitudes, multitudes in the valley of decision" (3:14 AV). Decisions can only be made when facts are to hand.[3]

Together we can win

It's a real battle and there are casualties and painful losses. Jesus said he was sending us out as lambs among wolves. If he was reviled and persecuted we must expect the same (Matthew 10:16/John 15:20). But the battle is not between Jesus and the devil, for there's no contest here: the Lord is always in control. At his lowest, when he laid aside heavenly power to become man, he won the day. In death he disarmed the devil and his hosts, leading them captive and making them subjects of mocking and ridicule (Colossians 2:15).

On the contrary, the battle is for the souls of men (Revelation 18:13). Don't lose sight of this. Our warfare is not for ourselves. We are secure. Born of the Spirit we work out our souls' salvation with fear and trembling (Philippians. 2:12). We have eternal life. We battle on behalf of others, as Jesus did, to put the power to choose life in their hands.

Together, evangelicals, social activists and charismatics present a formidable challenge to the one who holds men's souls in his web of lies and deceit. United, with the example of Jesus and the power of his Spirit, we oust Satan from his *heavenly* pedestal, expose him on *earth* and will see him cast into *hell* fire reserved for him and his angels. Bound together as a threefold cord, our strength is unbreakable. Our distinctives work side by side as a trident to see our enemy dislodged.

The chart below shows the reality of the tremendous power harnessed when Christians are united in diversity. I don't wish to over-simplify or typecast the streams but the more we flow together, the more we affirm one another's emphases, the more we become the "river whose streams make glad the city of God" (Psalm 46:4).

Notes

1. See Appendix 3 for notes on change within the Pioneer Network.
2. Global Focus website is – www.global-focus.org.uk
3. See note 1, p. 36.

STREAM	REALM	FOCUS	PRIMARY EMPHASIS	DISTINCTIVENESS	MAIN CONCERN	DESIRED OUTCOME
EVANGELICAL	HELL	SOUL	SALVATION	PROCLAMATION	TRUTH	WORD
SOCIAL ACTIVIST	EARTH	BODY	JUSTICE	CARE	PRACTICAL HELP	WORKS
CHARISMATIC	HEAVEN	SPIRIT	HEALING	MIRACLES	SPIRITUAL GIFTS	WONDERS
EMERGING APOSTOLIC	HELL EARTH HEAVEN	SOUL BODY SPIRIT	SALVATION JUSTICE HEALING	PROCLAMATION CARE MIRACLES	TRUTH PRACTICAL HELP SPIRITUAL GIFTS	WORD WORKS WONDERS

Note: Historically British evangelicals were concerned with social action – Wilberforce was evangelical. However, during the early part of the last century there was a negative reaction to the "social gospel." Since then evangelicals have been primarily concerned with biblical authority and preaching the word. This is changing as the Lord blurs the lines between the streams of truth. It is not my intention to create stereotypes; we don't fit neatly into boxes!

CHAPTER 22

IT'S BETTER CAUGHT THAN TAUGHT
– IT'S BETTER FELT THAN TELT

Church – the holy virus

The end is in sight. God's final shakings have begun. The church will emerge reshaped and revitalized to live her finest hour as God's agent for the kingdom. The questions which remain are – "What part will I play in the climax of history?" and "What part will those with whom I work and worship have in the grand finale?" The end is all about Jesus and his triumphant return to earth, first in Spirit among his people who prepare the way, then in flesh for every eye to see (Revelation 1:7).

What a privilege to call nations to their destiny in Christ and invite them to line the route of his return, welcoming the King of kings and Lord of lords to his rightful place as head of his church and governor of the universe. To achieve this honour and fulfill our calling to herald Christ's coming, we must nurture this fresh way of understanding church. We must allow the Spirit freedom to break habits and mindsets which keep us bound to old ways largely irrelevant in our world today.

We must see church as a holy virus to be "caught before it is taught." In the words of the old Scots saying, "It's better felt than telt." Once infected we'll never be the same again. Time is short, but God is not in panic mode. It takes only a remnant to return and rebuild Jerusalem (Nehemiah 1:3 AV/Haggai 1:14) or a Gideon's band of 300 battle-wise troops to bring down the hosts of Midian (Judges 7:7).

Fear and folly leave the few . . .

As with Gideon's main army, fear or folly can disqualify. Twenty-two thousand fighting men were dismissed because they trembled. Nine thousand seven hundred, who ran to drink with no thought of enemy presence, were also turned away. Only those who cupped their hands, watchful for danger, could be trusted. We too must persist beyond mere freedom from the paralysis of fear, to sharpen our awareness of the enemy and gain an irrepressible determination to win.

Only those who have felt God's passion for the world, his heartbeat for the lost, will participate in the big showdown. Talking the language of Zion is not enough: we must have seen the promised land. A story around at the time of that amazing Broadway musical *South Pacific* illustrates this point.

The demand for tickets left hundreds of people desperate. Some would travel thousands of miles to pick up a cancellation. The number of the disappointed grew every day and some could hardly face friends and family having to admit they'd failed to get a seat. Canny ticket touts plugged into this market. Scouring the theatre at the end of each performance they found ticket stubs and programmes to sell to these unfortunate folk who could go back with "evidence" to tell the story of what they'd "seen."

Sadly, there are Christians too who live on the experiences of others. They've got a programme and ticket stubs but they've never seen the show. With no real understanding, they're like tourists bustled from one important site to another without absorbing the atmosphere of the place. The memory soon fades and there's nothing to draw them back again. They are "virtual reality Christians," "almost" but "not quite." Jesus said "I am . . . the truth [the reality]" (John 14:6). Knowing him and sharing his longings are the only ways to stay engaged for the long haul, or in Bible speak – to "endure to the end."

What do you see?

The prophets lived on visions. Over and over they were questioned, "What do you see?" What they had seen motivated them. Their visions caused fire in their bones. They had no rest until they had accomplished their tasks. They were "seers." Now we, the church of Christ, are "seers." We are God's prophet, or prophetic people today and without vision we will perish (Proverbs 29:18) we will utterly fail to complete the work God has given us to do. So, how do we receive and nurture vision that will sustain us from youth even to old age? What is it that, once seen, will hold us together in all our diversity to run the race and finish the course?

Zechariah had a vision. The main theme of his prophecy is the second coming of Jesus. His name means "the Lord remembers" and has particular relevance for us. He is like the church, asleep and dreaming. The angel awakens him and demands, "What do you see?" (Zechariah 4:2). In his dreams he saw a solid candlestick of pure beaten gold.

Today the Holy Spirit shakes the church to awaken us. He has come to show us Jesus, the light of the world. Only a vision of Jesus gives us strength, courage and endurance to fulfil the great commission to reach all peoples with the good news. Jesus is the golden candlestick of beaten work in Zechariah's dream, a symbol of suffering divinity and illumination. It is Jesus, bruised and beaten, through whom the light of God shines in a dark world to lighten our lives. Every hammer-blow dent becomes a tiny mirror reflecting Father's love.

Those who see cannot be shaken . . .

This is the vision to keep alive: never lose sight of Jesus. As Elisha fixed his eyes on Elijah, determined to obtain a double blessing (2 Kings 2:9–14), and smitten Israelites gazed on the serpent of bronze lifted up in the wilderness (Numbers 21:8–9), so we fix our eyes on Jesus the author and finisher of our faith (Hebrews 12:2).

Those who fear the Lord have nothing else to fear, and those shaken by him can be shaken by nothing else. The psalmist knew this and exclaimed, "Those who trust in the Lord are like Mount Zion, which cannot be shaken but endures for ever" (Psalm 125:1). Campbell McAlpine, another father of the Charismatic renewal, repeatedly reminded us young would-be-leaders there are 365 "fear nots" in the scriptures, one for every day of the year!

Isaiah, when describing what he saw of the future, cried, "'Though the mountains be shaken and the hills be removed, yet my unfailing love for you will not be shaken nor my covenant of peace be removed,' says the Lord, who has compassion on you," (54:10). Quite the reverse of what he saw for the future of the world and its injustices: "I will punish the world for its evil, the wicked for their sins . . . I will make the heavens tremble; and the earth will shake from its place at the wrath of the Lord Almighty, in the day of his burning anger" (13:11–13).

As sure as the rising sun, God's judgements are coming. There's no escape. As Noah faced the earth-cleansing flood, we will face the purifying fire. However, we have an ark more secure than his trusty vessel and a future more bright than his brave new world to take us through the purging.

. . . they are a holy people . . .

Peter's second epistle warns in the last days scoffers will mock and question the promise of Jesus' coming. He continues:

> But they deliberately forget that long ago by God's word the heavens existed and the earth was formed out of water and by water. By these waters also the world of that time was deluged and destroyed. By the same word the present heavens and earth are reserved for fire, being kept for the day of judgement and destruction of ungodly men . . . The Lord is not slow in keeping his promise, as some understand slowness. He is patient with you, not wanting anyone to perish, but everyone to come to repentance. But the day of the Lord will come like a thief. The heavens will disappear with a roar; the elements will be destroyed by fire, and the earth and everything in it will be laid bare. *Since everything will be destroyed in this way, what kind of people ought you to be?* You ought to live holy and godly lives as you look forward to the day of God and speed its coming . . . But in keeping with his promise we are looking forward to a new heaven and a new earth, the home of righteousness (2 Peter 3:5–13, my italics).

. . . tested and tried in the fire

As Jesus baptizes us with the Holy Spirit and fire, and we receive his corrective judgements, nothing will remain for the final fires to burn. Paul confirms whatever we build on the foundation of Jesus will be tested, be it gold, silver, costly stones, wood, hay or straw. A man's "work will be shown for what it is, because the Day will bring it to light. It will be revealed with fire, and the fire will test the quality of each man's work" (1 Corinthians 3:13).

Later, concerning conduct at the Lord's Supper, he advises, "A man ought to examine himself before he eats of the bread and drinks of the cup . . . if we judged ourselves, we would not come under judgement. When we are judged by the Lord, we are being disciplined so that we will not be condemned with the world" (1 Corinthians 11:28–32). For us, God's judgements are remedial, they are life and health. For the unrepentant, sold out to wickedness, they are all-consuming.

What kind of people?

Those who have seen Jesus and understood that his testimony is the Spirit of prophecy (Revelation 19:10), will live holy lives, aware of the urgency of the days. Many Christians who feel they have revelation of the meaning of prophecy are arrogant and judgemental, which is out of character with Jesus and the Spirit of prophecy. They delight in knowledge rather than a change of heart that nurtures a fear of God and love for their fellow men. We must conclude that even if they are right, which is unlikely, they have missed the point.

If we know what is about to take place we should heed Peter's question – "*what kind of people ought you to be?*" (2 Peter 3:11, my italics). Having an understanding of prophecy will result in us being altogether different, a people representing Jesus in character and power. Perhaps he was referring to such a people when he said, "this generation will certainly not pass away until all these things have happened" (Matthew 24:34).

The generation of Jesus Christ . . .

Jesus is the last Adam and the first being of a totally new creation (1 Corinthians 15:45–49). Does it mean that the beginning of the generation he was referring to in Matthew 24:34 and all who are born of his Spirit are part of this "generation of Jesus Christ"? Verse 1 of Matthew's Gospel reads – "The book of the generation (Greek *genesis*) of Jesus Christ" (AV). We then have the 28 generations leading to his birth spanning 2,000 years. This is the record of those who, prior to Jesus' birth, were included in his *genesis* by faith.

The Gospels do not simply record Jesus' pedigree in history, they are also a prophetic statement of how this One, who never had a wife or sired a child, is "bringing many sons to glory" (Hebrews 2:10). They reveal the secrets of history future, from his resurrection over 2,000 years ago to the present day. These sons – you, me and all women and men who humbly bow to him – are the continuing generation that "will not pass away until everything is accomplished." This is the "chosen generation" Peter refers to (1 Peter 2:9, AV), who are kings and priests, the holy nation that belongs to God, carrying on the work Jesus began in the same Spirit of humility and power.

The candlestick Zechariah saw, symbolic of Jesus, is also a symbol of the church. This is seen in Revelation 1, where seven candlesticks are seven churches. Jesus plainly told his followers "You are the light of the world" (Matthew 5:14). Candlesticks in Bible times were fuelled by oil, the symbol of the Spirit as opposed to human power.

When we receive Christ and are baptized in the Holy Spirit we are connected to the same unending oil supply as Jesus. We share the gold of his divine nature and the power to illuminate this dark world. We too are a candlestick of beaten work and therefore will be bruised. Through persecution we will continue to reveal his dying love to the world.

. . . out in the open and on the move

What better place to close than the simple commission of Jesus to "let your light shine before men, that they may see your good deeds and praise your Father in heaven" (Matthew 5:16). These words sum up all we've been saying about the kind of church he is looking for today.

Let's desert our ghettos to be "a city set on the hill which cannot be hidden." Let's take our lamps from under the bowls and place them on the stand where they can be seen. Let's stop trying to tempt people into our buildings and break out to take the living building of our relationships to the people. Let's be a moving, mobile family on the road with Jesus where he spent his time and ministry. Let's join him where he is, rather than trying, unsuccessfully, to persuade him to join us where we are.

It is happening. The pillar of fire has moved and more of God's children are moving with it. God's "shaking" is stirring us from our dreams so we step into reality. It's make or break time and our reactions will determine whether we are part of Nehemiah's "remnant which returns." Not everyone will respond. Some prefer the dubious comfort of the ghetto to the excitement of the journey. But, for those who have ears to hear, there is a sound of marching feet as the tribes begin to gather for the final stage of our journey to the city whose maker–builder is God – the New Jerusalem, the mother of us all.

I leave you with Ronnie Wilson's great hymn, a product of that outpouring of the Holy Spirit which gave birth to the "House Church" movement in Britain, a movement which today faces the same challenge we accepted all those years ago. Will we continue as pioneers or will we yield to the pressures to settle? Pioneers or settlers: which will it be?

I hear the sound of rustling in the leaves of the trees,
The Spirit of the Lord has come down on the earth;
The Church that seemed in slumber has now risen from its knees,
And dry bones are responding with the fruits of new birth.
Oh, this is now a time for declaration,
The word will go to all men everywhere;
The Church is here for healing of the nations,
Behold the day of Jesus drawing near.

My tongue will be the pen of a ready writer,
And what the Father gives to me I'll sing;

I only want to be his breath,
I only want to glorify the King.

And all around the world the body waits expectantly,
The promise of the Father is now ready to fall;
The watchmen on the tower all exhort us to prepare,
And the Church responds – a people who will answer the call.
And this is not a phase which is passing,
It's the start of an age that is to come;
And where is the wise man and the scoffer?
Before the face of Jesus they are dumb.

A body now prepared by God and ready for war,
The prompting of the Spirit is our word of command;
We rise, a mighty army, at the bidding of the Lord,
The devils see and fear, for their time is at hand.
And children of the Lord hear our commission:
That we should love and serve our God as one.
The Spirit won't be hindered by division
In the perfect work that Jesus has begun.

Ronnie Wilson © Kingsway's Thankyou Music 1978
PO Box 75, Eastbourne, East Sussex
BN23 6NW (tym@kingsway.co.uk).
Used by permission.

EPILOGUE

12 February 1999

Bill Wilson arrived in the UK on Friday morning. His flight had been delayed and he'd been without sleep for 36 hours. He was due to speak at a church outside London that evening. I expected he would want to rest and prepare for his busy schedule but he insisted on spending time with Gerald Coates and me. I am profoundly grateful to Bill, and to the Lord, for this was a divine connection. During the drive from the hotel in Watford to meet Gerald at Waverley Abbey House in Surrey, Bill's remarkable story unfolded.

As a child Bill was abandoned in St Petersburg, Florida, by his mother who could no longer care for him. A Christian man picked him up and bundled him off to a Pentecostal youth camp where he went forward to give his life to Christ. Even here he met rejection. Because of his dishevelled appearance and smelly clothes no one wanted to pray with him. Nevertheless, he found God and determined to return to the street to reach children who had no knowledge of God's love or the truth that Jesus had died to set them free to have a relationship with him.

I'll never forget Bill's words, "I've spent 30 years becoming an overnight success!" No one wanted to know him when he was struggling to make his vision a reality. During those early years few believed in him. Now with a Sunday school of well over 20,000 kids every week and a church of 2,500 built, largely, from converted children, everyone is keen to hear his story and be known as his friend. All along Bill knew the only way to reach the thousands caught in the poverty trap was to take Jesus to them where they were. To build church among them and their families on the side-walk.

It was not an easy task and took years to win trust. Broken ribs, threatened with knives and shot at, were just some of the things Bill suffered. Perhaps the worst pain was to be misunderstood and marginalized by fellow-Christians. These hardships he shared in common with the first apostles and Jesus, who went to "that which was his own, but his own did not receive him" (John 1:11). Finally, all the persecution, hard work and prayers paid off as kids began to turn to Jesus. To date, hundreds and hundreds have yielded their lives to the Lord and are involved in the home church, all over the USA and beyond.

Today, success under his belt, Bill still drives a bus on Saturdays and teaches on the sidewalks while discipling fresh teams into the heart of Metro-Ministries. He lives at the warehouse, the base from which he conducts his work. On Sundays he travels to share the story and raise funds around the USA. There was a light in his eyes as he revealed that his is one of the few Christian works in the USA receiving money from Christians in other nations, some much poorer than America. For him, this support is recognition that he is reaching a downtrodden people who are mostly forgotten by the world's richest and most powerful nation.

As we talked I became more aware of the passion which drives this man in his mission to rescue children, not only from the streets of New York but also in major cities around the world. Tears filled Bill's eyes, "I don't know how long I've got. I've suffered a heart attack and with all I've been through I probably won't last much longer. I'm 50 now, but if God gives me 10 good years, I'll plant the seeds of side-walk Sunday school in the souls of Christians in many nations." And I knew he would. Whether he lived or died was irrelevant. The spark of his faith was already setting light to the dry tinder of saints longing to find ways to reach the edges of society and win the lost to Jesus.

As we motored back there was a hint of tiredness in those bright eyes. This was hardly surprising as he had been up for almost two days but this did not stop Bill telling me excitedly of his plans to invade Romania with the Good News. "The Swiss army are selling off military mobile bakeries. They can produce 200 loaves an hour. When we've shared Jesus with the street kids they can take the other kind of bread home." I remembered the words of William Booth, General and founder of the Salvation Army, "You cannot preach the gospel to a man with an empty stomach!"

I dropped this amazing man at his hotel in time for him to wash and prepare for the first meeting of his itinerary that would take him to Scotland and keep him in the UK for almost two weeks. Whatever else happened during his trip I knew I'd had a God appointment. This humble servant of the Lord had found a new way to be church in a world disillusioned with Christianity. He's one of the unstoppable generation that will not pass away until everything God planned has happened!

11 March 2001

I don't usually have dreams with any great significance. However, this Sunday morning I awoke in the early hours with the full colour stereo dream I'd had at the front of my mind. I was with a group of people gazing at a huge rock formation which, as a result of erosion, was beautifully smooth and the complex group of stones were finely balanced. It had been there for eons.

Around the rocks were massive buildings representing every institution in society, church included. Suddenly I cried, "It's going!" As I spoke the rocks slowly collapsed, setting off a chain reaction like the blast of a nuclear explosion. The effect was a line of falling dominos as, in quick succession, the buildings went down one after another. "The church is going too!" I cried. No sooner had the words left my mouth than a glorious cathedral-like structure was gone, nowhere to be seen. Not one stone was left standing on another – the devastation was complete; nothing remained.

FURTHER READING

Anderson, Neil T. and Saucy, Robert, *The Common Made Holy,* Monarch Books. Recently reissued as *God's Power at Work in You*

Banks, Robert, *Paul's Idea of Community*, Paternoster Press

Chevereaux, Guy, *We Dance Because We Cannot Fly*, Marshall Pickering

Cole, Graham, Hyton and Lewis, *What is the New Age?*, Hodder & Stoughton

Dixon, Patrick, *Futurewise,* HarperCollins.

Drane, John, *The McDonaldization of the Church*, Darton, Longman and Todd

Hyatt, Eddie L., *2000 Years of Charismatic Christianity*, Hyatt International Ministries, Inc.

Kang, C.H. and Nelson, Ethel R., *The Discovery of Genesis*, Concordia

Kelly, Gerard, *Get a Grip on the Future Without Losing Your Hold of the Past,* Monarch Books

Lamb, Henry, *The Rise of Global Government*, University of Texas.

Lyne, Peter, *First Apostles, Last Apostles*, Sovereign World

Manning, Brennon, *The Ragamuffin Gospel* Multnomah Books

Mills, Brian and Mitchell, Roger, *Sins of the Fathers*, Sovereign World

Moynagh, Michael, *Changing World, Changing Church*, Monarch Books

Nee, Watchman, *Further Talks on the Church Life*, The Stream Publishers

Nee, Watchman, *The Normal Christian Church*, International Students Inc.

Newbiggin, Lesslie, *The Household of God*, SCM

Noble, John, *First Apostles, Last Apostles*

Paterson, Dirk, *Cults and the European Union – a Reflection for UK Churches*, Christian Solidarity Worldwide

Schlink, Basilea, *New Age from a Biblical Viewpoint*

Scott, Martin, *For Such a Time As This*, Pioneer Direct

Scott, Martin, *Sowing Seeds For Revival*, Sovereign World

Seaton, Chris, *Identificational Repentance – Towards a Definition*, Peaceworks

Seaton, Chris and Ellis, Roger, *New Celts*, Kingsway

Simson, Wolfgang, *Houses that Change the World*, OM Publishing

Thwaites, James, *The Church Beyond the Congregation*, Paternoster Publishing

Willard, Dallas, *The Divine Conspiracy*, Fount

APPENDIX 1

MATTHEW 18 "BINDING AND LOOSING"

Dear John,

I think that you are right to emphasize the fact that this whole chapter is about reconciliation and restitution, not punishment or shaming people. The chapter begins with the sad fact that little ones can go astray. This is followed by the happier fact that God actively seeks those who wander off and he rejoices at their re-inclusion, rather like a farmer finding a lost sheep. After this comes the passage concerning the brother who sins against you. Here the emphasis is on our need to forgive and be merciful when we have been sinned against as in the parable of the unjust servant.

As R.T. France outlines in his book on Matthew's Gospel, binding and loosing would have naturally suggested to Jesus' hearers the way in which the rabbis made decisions that either bound people to certain actions or loosed them from certain obligations. For example, your teacher might bind you to tithe even your herbs, or loose you from this demand. This interpretation fits with the thrust of the chapter as we seek to define the terms for reconciliation and how the words of God/Jesus/Paul relate to different situations. There are reasons to see this as being in Jesus' mind when he used these terms.

Matthew 18:17 contains one of the two uses of "ekklesia" in the Gospels, the other being in 16:18. It was the common equivalent of "qahal" in the Old Testament and as such held many resonances for the early Christians. Qahal in Deuteronomy describes a non- (or not as yet!) institutionalized group who were the congregation of God at Sinai. This Sinai tradition recalls the close relationship between the formation of Israel and the giving of the Law in Exodus.

The similarity between newly constituted Israel and the newly constituted church is not difficult to see. Parallels are clear. Those who followed Yahweh now correspond to those who follow Jesus. Neither congregation was necessarily fixed or local; movement and change were key characteristics. Within this wilderness tradition the central elements are covenant, law and nationhood. The use of "ekklesia" in Matthew 18:17 with its Septuagint (Qaha) resonance, would actually fit well with Matthew's emphasis on the Law as having a central place in the life of the new Israel.

This raises issues about the authority of the Hebrew scriptures in the life of the church, which is a preoccupation in Matthew. The two passages mentioning ekklesia appear to give more authority to people than to scripture! In chapter 16:19 authority to "bind and loose" lies in the person of Peter and in chapter 18:18 it resides in the congregation.[1] Again this has Old Testament precedent.

The most frequent use of "ekklesia/qahal" is in Chronicles. Here it sometimes refers to a gathering of the leaders of Israel to make important decisions (1 Chron. 13:2–4). This has obvious parallels with the Matthew 18 passage, as the "ekklesia" can now gather to decide on individual cases. References to binding and loosing in both passages would have suggested to Matthew's readers that the church was taking on the rabbinical function of taking Torah and applying it in a given context. The technical term for this was "halakic midrash."

It would be unlikely that Jesus was suggesting the Sermon on the Mount, as intensified Torah, be discarded in favour of the rulings of the church! The church has to take Torah seriously.

Antinomianism is not a viable option. Yet this interaction between "two or three" and the Law shows the Law is not viewed as carefully refined rules. Rather it is speech to be empathetically understood, and embodied; it continually interacts with the community in which Jesus promises to be always present.

This dynamic interactional process discovers what is binding – or not – in specific cases (Matthew 18:18–20). Just as Jesus himself had to demonstrate wisdom in balancing justice and mercy in individual circumstances and just as Jesus contextualized Torah in the Sermon on the Mount, the church now continues this task. If this is a correct interpretation it has lots of current implications for us, particularly as we seek to deal with today's ethical challenges balancing holiness and mercy.

Richard Roberts, The Mill Church, East Coker, Somerset, UK.

Note

1. R.T. France suggests that this is an intentional dynamic – authority is between the two, the individual and the corporate, rather than resident in either one alone.

APOSTOLIC MINISTRY IN THE BIBLE

Section 1: Relating Apostolic Ministry to Our Own Context

This section is an attempt to look at apostolic ministry as portrayed in the New Testament and to relate this to our own situation today. Some of the statements that follow are probably well accepted but there is also a more theologically orientated Section 2 to examine some of the less evident assumptions in this first part.

Apostles and prophets as enduring ministries

In the Letter to the Ephesians the church is likened to a building with certain component parts. Jesus is the "chief cornerstone" of the building, the major part of the structure, but the apostles and prophets are indispensable and living supports for the building. Most commentators seem to take the "foundational" ministries of apostle and prophet in Ephesians 2, 3 and 4 to refer to New Testament figures. Paul writes that the gospel has "now been revealed to God's holy apostles and prophets." Notice the present tense in "now been revealed". These were not the now long dead Old Testament prophets who had spent at least 400 years in their graves! So it is clearly not the Old Testament prophets followed by the apostles in the New Testament that Paul has in mind.

Both the apostles and prophets are seen as relating to "the church" in an indispensable way, so that churches would fail to exist without their support. This makes it difficult to believe that the church has managed to exist throughout the centuries without the presence of both apostolic and prophetic figures. It seems most likely that they have still been around, despite our failure to recognize them; figures like John Wesley and George Fox spring to mind. Sadly, non-recognition is probably common for apostolic figures and certainly Paul spent a lot of time outlining and defending his own call to this ministry. The early chapters of his letter to the Galatians are a prime example of this.

Apostles and the authority that comes from God's call

The term "apostle" is primarily related to a certain sort of God-given authority. Apostolic ministry begins with a call from God. It is not a role that can be taken upon oneself without God's prior initiative. This role is attested by certain outcomes, like miraculous signs and patient suffering, along with the ability to create communities that are centred on Christ. Paul covers these points in his earlier letters, particularly in the Corinthian correspondence.

Apostleship comes out of encounters with God. It does not arise out of head knowledge or through study, however valuable these things may be. The 12 spent a lot of time with Jesus and Paul had a vision of the risen Christ. I think that the core of apostolic ministry is having "seen" something of Jesus (the gospel) and having been commissioned by God / Christ to communicate that revelation to people and to outwork it practically. Paul did this in his visits and his letters to churches. The apostles' teaching is therefore important – both the teaching of the 12 with their unique witness to Christ, but also apostolic teaching today – as that teaching creates church. It is in a real sense a communication of revelation that has been personally apprehended.

There is also an aspect to apostolic authority that relates to "the powers and principalities" of this present age (Ephesians 6). This could refer to either or both secular or spiritual powers, and therefore goes beyond what we traditionally think of the true sphere of influence for religious leaders in a modern secular society. For example, Paul was sent to speak before kings and rulers, and his presence in a city often caused shock waves that disrupted the current societal arrangements.

The authority of an apostle in a church or in an individual's life works primarily through relationship, rather than through a hierarchy. Hence, the family metaphors around apostolic relationships – Timothy as a son, Paul as a mother and father, etc. He had proven his care, faithfulness and his effectiveness in the past and he worked through a network of those with a clear respect for his proven worth. His authority was exercised with clarity and Paul was not afraid to confront those in positions of authority in local churches when they seemed to be going astray. He also actively placed people in positions of responsibility in the churches he had helped to found. But this authority was based upon the trust engendered by a life lived in conformity to the gospel. Obedience to Paul was based on relationship, persuasion and reason grounded in the gospel of freedom, not on his own arbitrary will.

Differentiating apostles and prophets

Apostles are foundational to the church, along with prophets. Apostles bring foundational teaching based on a prior revelation of Jesus. They convey "doctrine" – out of a life encounter with Jesus, not from a book on Systematic Theology!

Prophets bring revelation that is more situation-specific, such as that conveyed by the prophet John in Revelation. Prophets address issues like repentance, hope, passion and direction. Both sorts of revelation, apostolic and prophetic, are needed for the church to mature in stature and to thereby be effective in mission.

Pastors / Teachers have some overlap with apostles, but with less commissioned authority and possibly less personal revelation.[1] Apostles bear a sense of having grasped something of "the whole counsel of God." I suspect that pastors / teachers primarily pass on and contextualize apostolic teaching that they themselves have seen by the passing on of apostolic tradition.

The minor apostles

Paul was a major apostle but there were other figures in the New Testament who shared in this ministry. These were more "minor" apostles.

It is perhaps the case that we are unnecessarily reticent to call people "apostles" today because we use the term in a hallowed sense that somehow relates it to the unique place of the 12 or Paul. I suspect that quite a lot of people would fulfil the criteria of apostleship when less stringently defined.

These might be some of the characteristics of such a person:

i. He or she would have a particularly sharp perception of the Good News. They would have a clear and living sense of the presence of Jesus, the importance of his teaching and how he is relevant for us today.

ii. They would have an ability to create authentic church, albeit in new forms, and to forge community out of individual Christians. Their words and acts would be a foundation for the growth of an incarnational group of people, a body of Christ.

Paul expressed this goal when he said that he laboured towards the day when one church truly represented Jesus, "until Christ be formed in you".

iii. They would exhibit an authority that comes out of encounters with God where he has directed that person and thereby defined a specific commission. This person would know that they were sent to a particular situation or group of people. This might or might not be "sent" away geographically, but possibly sent by the call of God to engage with particular tasks and people.

For example, an extralocal apostle today could found churches or keep churches on track. This would be carried out in partnership with others, particularly by working with prophetic people. A more locally based apostolic figure might take the Christians around her and forge them into a community that engages powerfully in the work of God in the world. Without such a person groups of Christians can become directionless or overly religious – both of these possibilities are equally ineffective positions for mission.

Identifying leading figures in business or, say, human rights activists as apostles is attractive, as we have tended to underrate such people. However, in my understanding it does stretch the category a bit beyond the biblical evidence, although we would wish to esteem some of these people highly and support them in their own important calling. These callings will impact the world in vital and much needed ways.

It does not help to confuse apostolic and prophetic ministry or to call, for example, healing evangelists who act on a word of knowledge "prophets". We all need to pioneer in using the term apostle and the term prophet, where these are appropriate! If we fail to recognize God-appointed roles we will all miss out in the long term and be less effective at the work of God in the world.

Section 2. Theological Background to the Term "Apostle"

General comments

Whilst there has been a lot of research into biblical prophecy, there has been less research into the nature of apostolic ministry. One of the most helpful books that I have found is *Paul's Idea of Community* by Robert Banks (Paternoster Press).

It is important to decide what we stereotypically mean by the term apostle and not simply list characteristics of Paul that might not apply, say, to James, Philip or Barnabas. Paul is obviously our most available biblical example of an apostle, but it is difficult to justify labelling everything Paul did as characteristic of all apostles everywhere. There are things he clearly linked with his apostolic call – "the signs of an apostle" – and here we are on firmer ground. A phenomenological approach best fits the task, trying to get behind what the experience of being apostolic entails, rather than trying to overly define and restrict the meaning of the term. It is not desirable to define everything too precisely and God seems to have left us with a lot of untidiness!

In the New Testament the noun "apostolos" is applied only to individuals. There is good evidence that Paul and Barnabas worked in partnership and that there were others travelling with the apostles in the book of Acts. They were not loners and to read Paul's letters makes one aware of the diverse and in-depth relationships that he had with others. In modern terms we could say that he was an apostle with a team. Many of us have an ideological commitment to working in team as a biblical principle.

I prefer apostle plus team rather than "apostolic team" to

describe the structure of Paul's work. In our society there is a lot of suspicion of any relationship that clearly defined power implicates, such as calling someone an apostle or prophet. "Apostolic team" sounds very non-autocratic and is therefore attractive, even tempting!

A team can be defined by its function – a church planting team, or a team to care for the leaders of established churches, for example. One of these sorts of teams could be organized and led by an apostle. But the team itself is not necessarily "apostolic" in the sense that an individual is apostolic. Paul, not the team, was apostolic (called by God to the specific work); he was apostolic and others served the Lord by serving Paul in his task and thus at times were referred to as apostles. The biblical emphasis is on an individual being commissioned; only an individual can bear apostolic authority, not a team.

The linguistic background

Old Testament

In classical Greek the verb "apostellein", denoted being sent as *a personal representative of another* – a delegate or envoy with the full powers of the one who sent him. It could be used of a representative sent by a god. The noun apostole covered the situation in which one was a foreign ambassador. This person had a commission and was sent overseas.

The main Old Testament version of the early Christians was the Septuagint and they took and adapted words and concepts in their writings. In the Septuagint the noun apostole is used only once – in 1 Kings 14:6. Ahijah's prophetic denunciation of King Jeroboam is described and he is called "an apostle."

However, the verb is used hundreds of times. For example, in Isaiah 6:8 Isaiah hears God asking who shall he send to speak to Israel. But "send" here does not necessarily imply a translocal ministry (a sort of missionary) as Isaiah was sent from the presence of God to speak to his own people.

A simplistic approach to language comes up with spurious conclusions. An apostle was not necessarily "sent away" to another place – he was sent out from the presence of God or Jesus to do something on God's behalf. So the way the word group was used implies that being sent as a representative includes the authority to carry out a defined task. The way the word was used in the Septuagint would have influenced the way in which it was taken up afresh by the church.

Another important background to the use of the term in the New Testament is the Jewish institution of the *saliah*. This Aramaic term was used to describe a representative of another person with authority to act on his behalf – and it is thought by some to be behind the New Testament idea of the apostle, although not everyone agrees with this. This term was applied by the Jews in the early Christian centuries to figures such as Moses, Elijah and Ezekiel.

The terms "apostolos" in the Old Testament and "saliah" in Judaism both implied a limited commission, not an enduring office. This means that God could confer limited apostleship. Apostolicity has boundaries of people and of task. Peter was an apostle to the Jews, Paul to the Gentiles. Geography and demography are possible boundaries of operation.

New Testament background

The terms taken up for church leaders in the New Testament were adapted from other sources such as the Gentiles' fraternities ("episkopos") and the Jewish synagogue ("presbyteros") or from the Old Testament (the Septuagint – apostolos, prophetes).

As the word group apostello / apostole was carried over from the Old Testament it would have again suggested *unauthorized individuals who came to speak and act in a historical situation on behalf of God.* The core idea behind both prophetic and apostolic ministry is that of God sending an individual to a people group with a task in mind (such as Moses). The ministry of apostles, as well as prophets, is therefore charismatic rather than institutional. (Apostles, in the sense that I am using here, cannot be elected to office by the church. However, when a collection was made for the poor the men carrying the collection to Jerusalem were referred to by Paul as the church's apostles, 2 Corinthians 8:16–24, because they were people sent by the church to do a task. The term can have a wide meaning.)

One of the key factors in both prophetic and apostolic ministry would appear to be God's commission. Paul said that he was an apostle "by the will of God." Jesus' 12 original apostles were all called to be with him and then sent on a mission. Paul's call in Acts has many similarities with Old Testament precedents, particularly with the call of Jeremiah. There is an emphasis on speaking to kings and rulers in this call, Acts 9:15, as well as in Jeremiah chapter 1.

In the New Testament the term seems to denote three groups of apostles:

- The 12,
- post-ascension apostles who had been sent by Jesus,
- and the apostles of (sent by) the churches (2 Corinthians 8: 23).

This shows that the term was used loosely in some respects, with the context, as ever, determining the meaning of a word.

Are apostles and prophets the same?

It is necessary to give some attention to this question as recent writers, such as Wayne Grudem, have sought to conflate the ministries of the New Testament apostle and Old Testament prophet. It is perhaps important to realize that these terms may have been used rather loosely in New Testament times. As an example the Didache, which was probably written around 80–120 AD, seems to use the terms interchangeably.

Didache: "Of Apostles and Prophets."

> Every apostle who comes to you should be welcomed as the Lord, but he is not to stay more than a day, or two days if necessary. If he stays for three days he is a false prophet. And an apostle at his departure should accept only the provisions that will last him to his next night's lodging. If he asks for money, he is a false prophet.

However, there is an important difference between apostles and prophets. The defining characteristic of prophecy is ongoing oracular speech. Words claiming divine origin are the hallmark of prophecy. Prophecy is not usually doctrinal in its content.

Apostolic speech is more like that of Moses or Paul – revelation is received into the nature of the covenant between God and his people – the Law in the former case and Christ in the latter case. We could call this doctrinal, if we dissociate doctrine from the application of philosophical concepts to the action of God in the world and see it primarily as communication, something God has shown us about himself and his will.

Some early thoughts towards a biblical theology of apostleship

There have been many attempts to find a central theme for Old Testament theology. For example, books have been written suggesting that themes such as covenant, God's saving action, God's presence or a continuing dialogue between God and his people are the central theme of the Hebrew scriptures. It could actually be that there is no clear centre to Old Testament theology within the Hebrew Scriptures alone. The centre only becomes clear once Christ has appeared.

As Walter Brueggemann pointed out, Israel was held together as the people of God by three things:

- the priests who communicated the Law of God,
- a system of rituals and regulations ("the cults"),
- and the prophets who were sent by God to communicate his more immediate concerns.

When we come to the New Testament, the presence of Jesus makes it necessary for a new sort of leadership to come into existence, the apostle. There were some similarities between the New Testament apostles and the Old Testament prophets. Both received a commission from God / Jesus.

However there is an important difference between the prophet and the apostle. The prophets claimed verbal inspiration. The apostles, on the other hand, bore witness to Jesus, his life and his teaching. For example, Paul did not generally claim the authority of verbal inspiration in his writing, as did the prophets of Israel. I would suggest that this distinction between prophetic inspiration and apostolic witness holds true for us today in the Christian age. Paul's teaching, according to many scholars, was based on an extended reflection of the Damascus Road experience in which Christ was personally revealed to him. Apostleship does not require the verbal inspiration that prophetic ministry entails. Apostolic teaching is a witness to Jesus' life, death, resurrection and teaching. Hence the primacy of apostolic ministry (1 Corinthians 12:28).

The New Testament presents us with a theological centre, Jesus, for both the Old Testament and the New Testament. The people of God did not need an apostle in the same way in the Old Testament as we do, because apostleship relates to witness.[2] The apostles were bearers of the truth. But not truth in an abstract form – they were to be witnesses of a person who is the truth, Jesus. This also applies to the post-resurrection apostles who also were apprehended by a vision of Christ (or at least a vision of who Jesus is). They were certainly not just a bunch of church growth consultants! Apostleship was and is centred firmly in an appreciation of the gospel, a revelation of the risen Lord that urgently needs to be embodied in communities who thereby become church.

Richard Roberts, The Mill Church, East Coker, Somerset, UK

Notes

1. I am using "revelation" here not to mean new dogma, but in a broader sense of "seeing clearly." A depth of insight into Jesus, the kingdom of God and church might be in view here.
2. i.e. reporting what has been seen.

NOTES FROM PHILIP ISZATT'S TALK TO LEADERS 23 FEBRUARY 2001 ON THE CHANGES IN PIONEER

PASSION FOR MISSION AND THE SHAPE OF PIONEER

Ethiopia. A parable

55,000,000 people spread over a land mass 10 times that of the UK.

Most can eat only once a day, and then only meagrely. Ethiopia is the second poorest country in the world, and this year (2001) 12 million risk starving to death – up 50% on last year, because the rains have failed for the fourth year in a row!

Over the last few years help has poured in, but there is no real change. Why?

Well, 95% of Ethiopia's population are subsistence farmers, and they have a certain mindset.

Give an Ethiopian farmer grain and he will do one of two things – he will eat it or sell it. He will not save it to sow next year. Why? It is not because he is stupid or careless. He has two *good* reasons:

1. He *knows* some of his children will die next year, whatever he does. That is the way it has always been.
2. He *knows* that to plan for tomorrow means you have no faith in God. To save the grain for next year is to dishonour God!

Earth-resources satellite photography reveals a resource-rich country. There is even masses of water, underground. But every year millions starve to death.

The problem? Not lack of help, not politics, not the economy – these are effects rather than the cause. No, fundamentally the *cause* of the problem is the mindset of the subsistence farmer. God bless him.

I have the privilege of working with the largest evangelical/Charismatic movement in Ethiopia; the Kale Hewet church. Some 4,500,000 people in 4,300 congregations spread across the whole country. Perfectly positioned to bring real transformation to their country.

But first, the mindset of the church has to change.

At the moment Kale Hewet is centrally run with a political culture that disempowers 99% of its people. My privilege is to train its national leadership and then, through a cascading training plan using 613 trainers, for the Holy Spirit to change the mindset of all 4.5 million members to become change agents in their own communities. Even the course content of its 100 Bible Schools is being changed to support the project. We are four years into it, with another four to go. By 2005 we will have reached square one: the church beyond the congregation – the grassroots equipped and empowered to transform the nation.

But unless the mindset of the church changes nothing will happen!

So it is with Pioneer. *Sow a thought, reap an action.*

Why are we here?

Everything starts with this simple question: why are we here? What is Pioneer for, what is our destiny? What will not happen if Pioneer ceases to exist? How will we delay the kingdom if we do not do what God has called us to do?

I suggest: *we are **kingdom revolutionaries** – called to turn upside down all that is inside and outside the church that delays the King and the kingdom.* Essentially, we are revolutionaries.

If you agree with this, a second fundamental question arises: *how* will we fulfill this calling?

We share a revulsion. We are revolted by empire-building. Deep in our gut we believe that the man-made empires we see across the church carry the seeds of their own destruction. We even suspect that eventually such empires may form a barrier against the King.

We do not want to *be* an organization.

But, it's clear from 1 Corinthians 12:28 – where gifts of administration are listed with God's appointment to the church of apostles, prophets and teachers, etc – that organization can be godly and spiritual.

The metaphor behind the word *administration* here is of a boat being steered by someone's hand on the tiller. A gift of the Holy Spirit.

We do not want to *be* an organization. But we need to *have* one.

Unity vs agreement

Let me contrast the two ideas of unity and agreement.

"Unity" goes to the heart of empire, in which there is one centre that holds all the power, and vision, and draws into itself all the resources. Its greatest expression is in the production of obedient clones.

In contrast there is the biblical concept of agreement (very similar to *body*). "Agreement" refers to an orchestra of *different* instruments playing together in rich harmony.

These two words describe completely opposite political cultures in an organization. Though we find the first throughout Christendom, it is in fact worldly.

Jesus (in Matthew 20) knew that in just a few months *thousands* would be looking to his disciples for leadership. He also knew that they had grown up knowing only the leadership model of their Roman occupiers. In verse 20 we see the beginnings of that spirit of empire attempting to infiltrate the kingdom as James' and John's mother seeks advantage for them. It is this that prompted Jesus to say: "You know that the rulers of the Gentiles lord it over them, and their high officials exercise authority over them. Not so with you. Instead, whoever wants to become great among you must be your servant, and whoever wants to be first must be your slave – just as the Son of Man did not come to be served, but to serve . . ." (Matthew 20:25–26)

To be an orchestra of *different* instruments playing together in rich harmony is only possible if we allow the Holy Spirit to remove the spirit of empire from us.

Difference, from God's point of view, is the reason to be together. If your differences separate you, you are almost certainly in the flesh.

The reason for the fragmentation of the body of Christ, and disempowerment of the saints from the fourth century, is because we adopted unitary organization and leadership, instead of agreement.

Machines vs plants

Two theories of organization stand out. One sees organization as a machine, the other as a plant.

Let me tease out the differences between the two:

Question	Machine-type organization	Plant-type organization
1. Where is the life-force?	In the engine. The levers, wheels and pulleys are essentially inert (dead).	In every part.
2. Where is the life-design (the vision, the blueprint, the DNA)?	In the engineer, only.	In every part.
3. How is energy delivered?	A lever puts pressure on a wheel, a wheel puts pressure on a pulley, which puts . . .	By osmosis. By the sharing of permeable cell walls.
4. Where does value lie?	In what drops off the end of the production line, only.	In the self-sustaining nature of the life-force.
5. What causes growth and reproduction?	Sales department quotas!	The miraculous combining of the life-design and life-force *in every part*.

Fire and water

Pour water on a desert and you get a garden. Pour water on a machine and you get a junkyard.

Burn a forest, and you regenerate organic life. Burn a machine and you get a pile of ashes.

I suggest we want to have a plant-type organization.

So, what is the purpose of leadership?

While preparing this I had a nightmare. I dreamt I was no longer a church leader; God didn't want leaders any more – they were a *bad* thing. I was back in my first job; my nightmare was I couldn't do it.

Waking in a sweat, I asked God "Do you really want no leadership in the church?" "I want leadership", I heard him say, "but of a particular sort."

I didn't like the dream, but I think it was from God.

What sort of leadership does God want? One that creates an environment conducive to *life*.

Commanders vs facilitators

In all the theories about leadership, two models stand out.

The first is called **Command and control**, and in it all power vision and decision-making is centred on one place or person, and these travel in one direction only; from the centre outwards. In it a leader essentially uses other people to help her/him achieve *her/his* objective.

The second is **Facilitation**. A facilitator helps other people achieve *their* objectives. It takes time, patience, and an over-whelming desire to serve rather than be served.

(Of course, at times the facilitator/leader or discipler may give strong direction to new disciples who have voluntarily submitted themselves to her/his leadership as, indeed, Jesus did. J.N.)

Command and control is relatively easy, quick and cheap. Facilitation is hard, slow and costly.

Command and control produces passive people who are inward-looking, exclusive and conservative. Facilitation produces bold people who are outward-looking, inclusive and innovative.

I suggest we want to have a plant-type organization led by facilitator-leaders, in every part of Pioneer.

The three freedoms

With all this in mind, Pioneer wants to offer three radical freedoms to its ministries and churches:

1. The freedom to make significant relationships outside as well as inside of Pioneer
2. The freedom to enter into apostolic relationships of your choice that cause effective mission to occur.
3. The freedom to channel your resources to where you receive life.

Taken together, these are very radical indeed, very unusual, and are obedient to Matthew 20.

They set up the *possibility* of three sets of vital kingdom relationships which I would like to outline. But first let me set out the basis of these relationships if they are to honour God and be of use to him.

Voluntary mutual submission

The New Testament standard for all kingdom-relationships is **Voluntary mutual submission**. This applies person to person, person to organization, and organization to organization.

Voluntary, in that no one has permission from God to impose their will on another.

Mutual, in that we do (and must) need each other, in every case.

Submission, in that both parties strongly desire to be persuaded by the other.

If you move outside of voluntary mutual submission you move out of the spirit, and into the flesh. That is why empire-building has the seeds of its own destruction already in place.

The three sets of *potential* relationships I see are set out below. Please don't read into them "UK", because the body is international. And please don't read into them permanence, because they only describe a stage on the journey to one church with city-wide apostolic teams.

1. Internal Pioneer relationships:

Leadership			**Movement**
Vision	→	←	Vision
Model	→	←	Application
Facilitation	→	←	Resources
Ministry			**Church**
Strategic input	→	←	Context
Model	→	←	Credibility
Facilitation	→	←	Resources
Apostolic team			**Church/ministry**
Equipping	→	←	Resources
Model	→	←	Support
Facilitation	→	←	Relationship

2. External Christian relationships:

Pioneer church			**Non-pioneer church**
Relationship for territory	→	←	Relationship for territory
Pioneer ministry			**Non-pioneer ministry**
Relationship for territory	→	←	Relationship for territory
Pioneer movement			**Other movement/denom.**
Relationship for territory	→	←	Relationship for territory

3. External "secular" relationships:

Individual Christian			**Workplace/street, etc.**
Expand "church" into whole of life	→	←	Expand life into whole of church
Church/ministry			**Community/Social Agency**
Transform social structures	→	←	Opportunity for relevance
Movement			**Governments/Nations**
Make goodness fashionable	→	←	Provide opportunities to serve

Of course none of these will just happen. They are counter-culture. They will take effort and determination, grace and humour, guts and . . . guts. But if they become real we could say the Kingdom is on its way!

How will apostolic teams work?

At the heart of this facilitator-led, plant-type organization is the apostolic team, and the question on all our lips is: how will they work?

Difficult question. Our strong conviction is that there will be *several* models, and in order to avoid restricting variety we have tried not to be prescriptive. But there are some defining statements that we can make about them.

First, they'll work by voluntary mutual submission, which is far more revolutionary than it sounds.

Then, we can say they will not have positional power, because churches and ministries will choose them. They will have relational influence only.

Also, there will not be a formula by which they work.

They will facilitate; that is, they will help *you* to achieve *your* God-given objectives, rather than use you to achieve theirs. Again, this is far more revolutionary than it sounds.

And lastly, they will infect rather than instruct. They will be models, not moguls.

For what purpose?

Clearer than all this though is the *purpose* of apostolic teams. I suggest they will succeed if they:

1. Cause us to be effective in mission, and
2. Keep us "kingdom revolutionaries"; stopping us deteriorating into institutional church.

These are their two purposes, their raison d'etre.

Gerald Coates' leadership

To support the role of apostolic teams and the other internal Pioneer relationships I have outlined above, we need Gerald Coates and his team to lead us. They will model for us leadership that creates an environment conducive to life.

Clearly there will be some form around this leadership, though I would think it best to always consider its form as our best approximation to what the Holy Spirit wants at this stage. As soon as it is in concrete and can't be changed, we're dead.

Biblically, elders sit on the perimeter of a space. They do not occupy the space; they define it and make it safe. In fact, they create an environment conducive to life. At this time this means two main activities for Gerald and his team: (i) envisioning tomorrow and (ii) facilitating change today.

In both I think they will *facilitate*. They will usually not be the *origin* of vision or change; they will receive input, compile it and make sense of what God is saying to us all. So our expectations of them should not be that they will be telling us what to do; we must not force them to be command-controllers of a machine-type organization. That is not on their heart (though it is probably still in our expectation).

But be careful; none of this means there will be no leadership! We need *biblical* leadership. And when the last vestiges of empire leave our perception, the absolute need for accountability, submission, transparency and all the other body behaviours will become very clear. Voluntary mutual submission calls us to maturity, so that we are ready for Almighty God to use us as kingdom revolutionaries.

What are the keys to this radical new shape?

To achieve this new shape three things are needed in each of us:

1. Guts. This change is so unusual that people will keep on mis-understanding it, and subconsciously revert to previous ways. So we will need guts. We will not be able to have any sacred cows. Taking risks will need to be normal, and some mistakes inevitable – there is only one way for a company to avoid bad debts, and that is not to trade at all!

2. Vision-led. Whatever the practical shouts at us, we must stay vision-led at all times. What we are seeking to do is revolu-tionary, and the culture around us will try to force us back into the institutional mould.

3. Relationships. We will not be able to make external relation-ships that God can use unless, at the same time, we strengthen internal ones. I need to feel your hand gripping mine tighter as I reach out to make history. (This does not necessarily mean more time commitments; perhaps less, but expressions of love and respect are essential. J.N)

This is dangerous, isn't it?

Yes, very.

The two opposite dangers I see are that either nothing happens really – it all stays a lot of hot air. Or, personal empires will shoot up all over Pioneer and strangle us to death.

Between these I see the dangers of isolation, fragmentation or independence.

One thing is sure; freedom always shows up true character. We will be finding out what is *really* inside us over the next two years or so.

How will we know if the whole "project" has worked?

I would suggest each person in Pioneer, each ministry and each church apply the following five criteria to themselves, say once a year:

1. Do more of us know our "field" and are reaching it with the gospel?
2. Are more people being discipled?
3. Do more of us know our calling and are giving our lives to it?
4. Is the connection between personal and body calling closer?
5. Do we have more and stronger relationships outside and inside Pioneer?

If we use these questions well we will know, personally and as a movement, whether our change is succeeding or not. It will show us if Passion for Mission has really been released in us.

Ready?

This change is about moving from theory to application, from words to action, from obligation to freedom, and (relative) ineffectiveness to effectiveness.

Are you ready? Because the start date is today. God bless you with revolution. Philip Iszatt.